DISRUPT
AGING

DISRUPT
AGING

A BOLD NEW PATH TO LIVING
YOUR BEST LIFE *at* EVERY AGE

Jo Ann Jenkins

CEO *of* AARP

with Boe Workman

PUBLICAFFAIRS
New York

TO MY CHILDREN, CHRISTIAN AND NICOLE,
who inspire me to disrupt aging so they will be able to choose
how they want to live and age as they grow older.

PublicAffairs books are available at special discounts for bulk purchases in the U.S. by corporations, institutions, and other organizations. For more information, please contact the Special Markets Department at the Perseus Books Group, 2300 Chestnut Street, Suite 200, Philadelphia, PA 19103, call (800) 810-4145, ext. 5000, or e-mail special.markets@perseusbooks.com.

Library of Congress Cataloging-in-Publication Data
Names: Jenkins, Jo Ann, author.
Title: Disrupt aging : a bold new path to living your best life at every age
    / Jo Ann Jenkins, CEO, AARP with Boe Workman.
Description: First Edition. | New York : PublicAffairs, 2016. | Includes index.
Identifiers: LCCN 2016002025 (print) | LCCN 2016003527 (ebook) |
    ISBN 9781610396769 (hardback) | ISBN 9781610396776 (ebook)
Subjects: LCSH: Older people. | Aging. | Older people—Societies and clubs. |
    Self-actualization (Psychology) in old age. | BISAC: FAMILY & RELATIONSHIPS /
    Aging. | SOCIAL SCIENCE / Gerontology. | SELF-HELP / Aging.
Classification: LCC HQ1061 .J46 2016 (print) | LCC HQ1061 (ebook) | DDC
    305.26—dc23
LC record available at http://lccn.loc.gov/2016002025

Editorial production by Marathon Production Services. www.marrathon.net

Book design by Jane Raese

FIRST EDITION

10 9 8 7 6 5 4 3 2 1

CONTENTS

INTRODUCTION

Why Disrupt Aging? 1

CHAPTER 1

The New Reality of Aging 11

CHAPTER 2

Own Your Age 33

CHAPTER 3

Design Your Life 51

CHAPTER 4

Take Control of Your Health 73

CHAPTER 5

Choose Where You Live 103

CHAPTER 6

Finance Your Future 131

CHAPTER 7

Put Your Experience to Work 157

CHAPTER 8

Let's Change the Rules 181

CHAPTER 9

A New Vision for Living and Aging in America 209

JOIN THE CONVERSATION 217

TAKE ACTION 219

LEARN MORE: RESOURCES 239

ACKNOWLEDGMENTS 243

NOTES 247

ABOUT THE AUTHOR 265

Why Disrupt Aging?

The idea of living a long life appeals to everyone,
but the idea of getting old doesn't appeal to anyone.
—ANDY ROONEY

It wasn't just any birthday—it was my fiftieth birthday. And as my husband, Frank, and I entered the beautiful dining room of the Ritz-Carlton in Tysons Corner, Virginia, I was feeling a little impatient, even a bit on edge. I had left the dinner arrangements to Frank, something I normally don't do. The maître d' led us through the dining room to a small table in the back. "There was a bit of a mix-up with the reservation," he said, apologizing as he seated us at a small table near the entrance to the kitchen. I'll admit, I was annoyed. *This is just great,* I thought to myself. *My husband brings me to this elegant hotel to celebrate my birthday, and we're going to have to put up with all the banging from the kitchen and staff constantly pushing past.* A few minutes later the maître d' returned and said he had again made a mistake and was moving us to a separate room. By this point I had resigned myself to our culinary fate and was determined to just enjoy dinner with my husband, so we got up and followed him back through the restaurant into a different room. When the doors swung open, I was amazed and delighted to be greeted by about thirty of my dearest friends and colleagues. My daughter, Nicole, was there, and Frank had even arranged for our son, Christian, to come home from college to attend the celebration.

We had an absolutely wonderful time. As I sat there talking to my family and friends (who were all so proud of themselves for keeping the secret from me), I thought to myself, *Life doesn't get any better than this.*

Then I started opening my birthday cards.

> Happy 50th—You're now officially over the hill!

and

> Welcome to the "Over the Hill Gang"—
> Happy 50th Birthday!

and

> Think of it this way: you're not losing it—
> you're just not using it as often.

and

> Turning 50—Don't worry: You've still got it. So what if you
> can't remember where it is? Happy 50th Birthday!

At first I didn't think much about it. These cards are part of the ritual of turning fifty, right? We make fun of people's age, call them old. It's all done in a spirit of fun and adoration . . . isn't it? It is, of course, but still, I couldn't help but feel uneasy in that moment—and for days after. I felt really good about turning fifty, celebrating with my friends, and being happy about where I was in life. But when I read those cards it occurred to me that hidden within them was a not-so-subtle cultural ethos that didn't fit at all with what I—and most of my contemporaries—felt. I didn't feel old. I wasn't over the hill; I was on top of the mountain. I liked being there and planned on enjoying it for a while. In fact, I was already beginning to think about what mountain I might climb next. And I knew that I wasn't the only one who felt like that. In fact, as I thought about the people who were in the room celebrating my birthday with me, I could identify many who had long ago passed their fiftieth birthdays and were achieving great things—starting companies, setting new goals, finding new passions, or reigniting old ones. We are nowhere near slowing down.

I decided then and there that I wouldn't be defined by my age any more than I would be defined by my race, sex, or income. I want people to define me by *who* I am, not *how old* I am, and I refuse to allow the old expectations of what I should or should not do at a certain age define what I am going to do. I feel good about where I am in life, and I bet you do, too. So instead of just accepting and perpetuating the stereotypes or apologizing for our age—or denying it—let's embrace our age and make the most of it, shall we?

Shortly after my fiftieth birthday, and with my newfound determination, I decided to really own my age and follow my own path. Little did I know at that time that I would be leaving my job as COO of the Library of Congress to join AARP or

that my future work at AARP would allow me the perfect opportunity to help effect change not just in my life but in that
of many others. Talk about opportunity hitting you right on
the head!

I'll be the first to admit that this was not easy. The negative stereotypes of aging are so ingrained in our society and
personal identities, they are difficult to overcome. So most
of us don't even try. We either just accept it, thus perpetuating the negative image, or, as is increasingly common, we
simply deny that we are aging and fight against it with all
(the energy and money) we've got.

But I'll also tell you that it was incredibly satisfying. When
I made the decision to leave the Library of Congress to join
AARP, I was surprised by how many people were confused
about why I would leave a job I so dearly loved and was good
at to start a totally different career in a completely different
field at age fifty-two. But it made perfect sense to me.

This was the next chapter in my well-established five-year
planning cycle. I had always said I wanted to run a nonprofit.
But I never dreamed I'd end up running one as meaningful
as the AARP Foundation or that I would eventually become
the CEO of AARP, one of the largest nonprofit organizations
in the world. As I think back, it was one of those "be careful
what you ask for" moments. Never in my wildest imagination did I ever expect that I would be able to influence and
impact my own thinking on aging, much less that of millions
of others. When I think about the millions of people in this
country whose lives could be positively affected just by the
way we view and talk about aging, it's mind blowing. And
the only time I really thought about my age was to wonder
whether I was even old enough to be a member of AARP!

Our ability to live longer, healthier, more productive lives is one of mankind's greatest accomplishments. But aging is also one of life's great contradictions. It's everyone's dream to live to a ripe old age, but many people fear growing older. Aging is often viewed as more of a problem than an accomplishment. We live in a world that worships the fantasies of youth, yet we are being driven more and more by the realities of age. And those realities are changing rapidly and dramatically.

That's why, since becoming AARP's CEO in September 2014, I've been on a mission to disrupt aging. With the help of people around the country who are ready to change the conversation about what it means to get older, we've built a massive and growing movement around this idea. It's not about aging; it's about living.

We've all seen those ads on TV and in magazines: "Fifty is the new thirty" or "Sixty is the new forty." Although that may sound like a nice sentiment, as someone over fifty, I don't agree at all. Fifty is the new fifty—and I, for one, like the looks of it.

We're not becoming younger as we get older. We can't, no matter how much we may try. Instead, let's redefine what it means to be our age. I don't want to be thirty again—do you? Sure, I may sometimes think I'd like to *look* like I'm thirty and *feel* like I'm thirty, but I've benefitted immensely from the experiences and wisdom these years have brought me, and I wouldn't trade them for anything.

Today people fifty and older face distinct challenges and have different goals from people in their thirties and forties. We're at a different place in our lives, and we're motivated by different things. Because of our life experiences, we see the world through a lens shaped by experiencing the ups and downs of life, by the wisdom gained from those experiences, and by the comfort that comes from having a better understanding of who we are as individuals and what we want from life.

My years at AARP have confirmed for me that a growing number of people fifty and older are saying the same thing: We like where we are. We're looking forward to the years ahead. We are not looking back longingly on days gone by. We're connecting with more people in more meaningful ways through technologies. We're committed both to family *and* energized by work. We don't have to make a choice. We can—and should—have both.

We are caregivers, whether as adult children caring for older parents, parents taking care of children, grandparents taking care of grandkids, or some combination of all of these. We are volunteers and philanthropists. We are leaders in our communities, supporters of our churches, helping hands to our neighbors and friends.

We are a generation of makers and doers who have a desire to continue to explore our possibilities and to celebrate discovery over decline. We seek out opportunities and grab hold of them when we find them.

People fifty and older are still living in ways that reflect the attitudes, activism, and aspirations of the boomer generation. That optimism—that desire to live life on our own terms, to make a difference, to change the world—is very real. It confirms my belief that no one's possibilities should be limited by their age and that experience has value.

But I also know that people face real challenges every day. Many struggle to meet their most basic needs—health, financial, caring for themselves and their families. They don't want these challenges to limit or defeat them. They want to win back their opportunities.

We need to disrupt aging to help people confront their challenges and embrace their opportunities to the fullest extent possible. That requires changing the way we talk about aging from something we fear to something we look forward to.

Last year, when AARP joined with six other prominent aging organizations to gain a deeper understanding of the assumptions and thought processes that inform people's attitudes and judgments about aging, we found that the public largely holds an aspirational model of aging. People want to be self-sufficient, stay active, build intimacy with family and friends, and just have fun. But they are being held back because of the dominant cultural view of aging as a process of deterioration, dependency, reduced potential, family dispersal, and digital incompetence.

Our report concluded that "these deep and negative shared understandings make the process of aging something to be dreaded and fought against, rather than embraced as a process that brings new opportunities and challenges for individuals and society."

This is important because this negative understanding and, subsequently, the negative stories we tell ourselves and each other create for each of us individually and as a society a fatalistic reality of aging. The view of aging as decline becomes a self-fulfilling prophecy.

So let's change this—it's long overdue. Change the conversation and you change the reality. To start, there are three areas where change is most needed for individuals and in our society: health, wealth, and self.

First, we need to begin to focus on physical and mental fitness instead of diminishment, on preventing disease and improving well-being instead of just treating ailments. We need to help people feel empowered to become an active partner in their health care instead of being a dependent patient.

We also need to understand that wealth doesn't mean becoming rich beyond your wildest dreams; it does mean having financial resilience to not outlive your money. An active, engaged, employed older population has the potential to be more of an economic boom than a social challenge, such that the growing number of older people is not a drain on society but rather a key driver of economic growth, innovation, and new value creation.

Corporations, entrepreneurs, and small businesses are finally beginning to view the aging population as an opportunity—a growing market for goods and services, a pool of untapped talent and resources, and a driving force behind economic and social innovation—instead of an unaffordable cost and financial burden.

Finally, we must change the way we view ourselves and our inner lives from aging as decline to aging as continuous growth. Many older people feel cast aside. Instead, it's important that they develop a sense of purpose and positive self-image. The goal is to gain confidence in navigating life transitions—and see ourselves as integral parts of society—rather than being isolated from society.

I wrote this book to help us accomplish these goals. By focusing on health, wealth, and self, *Disrupt Aging* will begin to alter the mindset around aging. To begin, I will spend some time laying out the landscape. Aging has changed, and it's important to understand where we are today, where we must go, and how to take advantage of the incredible opportunities we now have to change the way we live our lives for the better. Then I'll be back to pick up the story.

You'll see that three themes run through this disrupt-aging discussion. First, we can't do this alone; we have to bring all of society with us. There is a public role for government at all levels, a private role for businesses and organizations, and a personal role and responsibility for each of us. Second, innovation—not just in terms of products and services but also in our social structures and programs—is the key to both individual and societal efforts to disrupt aging. And finally, disrupting aging is not just about people fifty and older; it affects people of all generations, and people of all generations need to get involved to make this change happen.

I hope *Disrupt Aging* will spark a movement that will change the conversation around aging in this country. Fortunately the movement has already begun. As the boomers move into their fifties and sixties, they are disrupting aging every day, just as they have done in every other phase of their lives. Millennials are also disrupting aging by the way they are demanding work-life balance in their jobs and how they are showing us the benefits of a shared economic model and shared communities. In these pages you will meet some of the people who are already making their mark as disruptors, and I hope you will be as inspired by them as I was.

We live in a very exciting time. Most people turning fifty today can expect to live another thirty-plus years. That's more time than they spent in childhood and in adolescence, and for many, it's more time than they spent working.

I believe we can create a society where all people can grow older knowing they have access to the care, information, and services they need to lead healthier lives with independence and dignity; where they have the financial resources and opportunities to match their longer life expectancy; and where they are seen as an integral and inspirational asset to society.

Maya Angelou once said that at fifty, each of us becomes the person we always wanted to be. I think that's true. I believe that age and experience can expand the possibilities in life for every member of society.

When we disrupt aging and embrace it as a part of life to look forward to, we can begin to discover the real possibilities of living the life we have always wanted. I hope you will join me on this journey.

CHAPTER 1

The New Reality of Aging

Aging is not "lost youth" but a new stage
of opportunity and strength.

—BETTY FRIEDAN

Make no mistake about it: America is aging. This is the transformational issue of our time. Its impact on the economy, jobs, education, culture and communities is pervasive. Just as the birth of the baby boom generation redefined American life in the 1950s, '60s, and '70s, the aging of the boomers will reshape the way we live and work in the 2010s, '20s, and '30s.

People today live longer and live better than ever before. Consider that two hundred years ago most of our ancestors were living at—or just above—subsistence level: farmers trying to eke out a living, village smiths, shoemakers, or craftsmen. If they developed diabetes, they would go blind and probably die early. If their eyesight started to give way as they reached middle age, they had to give up reading. Often a simple infection meant death. Meat was a rare luxury for most people. And instead of struggling to eat fewer calories as we do today, they fought to get enough to eat.

We have made phenomenal progress. Today most of us enjoy better health and a longer life than the wealthiest people in the wealthiest countries did just a century ago. And barring any catastrophic surprises in the first half of the twenty-first century, much of the world will come to share the long healthy life that is now enjoyed by the contemporary middle class in advanced countries.

The progress humanity has experienced over the last two centuries has no precedent. We can attribute this unparalleled progress largely to two factors. First, ours is the first age in which technological and material gains have been enjoyed by more than just a fraction of the population. It used to be that material gains were available to only the wealthiest in society—5 to 10 percent—while the rest of the population remained at mere subsistence levels.

Secondly, we have developed mechanisms for widely distributing information, knowledge, and wisdom. One hundred years ago a massive paper shortage and rationing along with the lowered purchasing power of the middle class (both the result of World War I) made information dissemination a challenge. Today, through mediums like television and social media, information is shared with all levels of society at incredible speeds. Fully 23 percent of the world's population is connected to the Internet. By 2020 that's expected to grow to 66 percent—5 billion people. Here in the United

States virtually everyone who wants to be on the Internet is connected.

It's an incredible time to be alive. In the United States we achieved a life expectancy of seventy about a generation ago. From the beginning of the modern calendar to 1900, life expectancy increased each year by an average of three days. Since 1900 it has increased by an average of 110 days a year. We added more years to average life expectancy in the last century than in all previous history combined.

In 1900 average life expectancy was forty-seven. Today it's seventy-eight, and if you make it to age sixty-five, you can expect to live about nineteen more years.

For the first time in history long life isn't a rarity. If you're fifty, you have half of your life ahead of you. Over half of the people born today will live to be one hundred. By 2030 people age sixty-five and older will number over 71 million and comprise nearly 20 percent of the population. The fastest growing age group is people eighty-five and older. By 2040 people aged sixty and over will outnumber children for the first time in the history of the world. This new longevity is one of the great success stories of the twentieth century.

Living Longer and Living Better

The new reality is that we're not just living longer; we're also living better. We're not tacking on more years of physical and mental decline at the end of life; in most cases we're adding more years of healthy and productive living. This concept of "healthy aging" was once thought to be an oxymoron. At the beginning of the twentieth century acute infectious diseases such as tuberculosis, smallpox, diphtheria, teta-nus, and others accounted for 80 percent of all deaths. By the 1970s the death rate from these diseases had been reduced by nearly 99 percent, and thus chronic diseases—heart disease, stroke, cancer, diabetes—became the major illnesses. As medical science increasingly prolonged life and then began to develop interventions for those diseases as well, the conventional wisdom was that the extra months and years resulting from those treatments would be spent in ill health and that although advances in medicine and public health could extend life, they could not delay the onset of chronic degenerative diseases.

Then in 1978 Dr. James Fries, a professor of medicine at Stanford University, hypothesized that if we could shorten the time between the onset of chronic illness or disability and the time in which a person dies, we could minimize the number of years people suffer, enabling them to live more successful and productive lives, which would benefit both them and society. This "compression of morbidity" theory, as he called it, revolutionized the concept of aging. Instead of merely accepting a gradual decline as inevitable, we began to focus on how to delay that decline through prevention, lifestyle changes, and health improvements aimed at pushing back the onset of morbidity.

We began exercising, joining fitness clubs, forming walking groups. We saw an explosion of research on nutrition. It seemed like a new diet appeared every week, and self-help books flooded the bookstores, telling us all the things we could do to "combat aging." At the same time, public health campaigns to reduce smoking, promote preventive measures, and encourage people to get health screenings such as mammograms have further helped people to live healthier and longer. And innovations in medical care, such as joint replacements and better methods for controlling diabetes, have helped to push healthy living even further.

This combination of a longer life expectancy and compressed morbidity means that the transition into what we used to call old age is redefining how we live our lives. And its impact is felt not by a relatively small percentage of our population but by millions. This, combined with the sheer numbers of aging baby boomers, is disrupting the traditional demographic shape of our society. Think of it this way: we used to depict the age of our population as a triangle, with the largest number of young people at the base and a declining number of older people toward the tip. Now the triangle has become a rectangle and is even beginning to invert, with more people at the top than at the bottom. Older is the new normal, and this is not only changing what it means to age but changing how we live, permanently altering the courses of our lives.

Redefining Our Life Course

These huge demographic shifts happen very rarely in our society. In the latter part of the eighteenth century, for example, we began to further define and refine stages of life. We began by creating the concept of "childhood." Up until that time children were considered little adults. Boys became adults either by entering the workforce or getting married. If he could do adult work, he was an adult. If he couldn't, he remained a child. There was no in-between. Then, at the turn of the twentieth century, "adolescence" was born, bringing us high school and the concept of the modern teenager. In the 1950s and early '60s a new life stage called "retirement" was introduced.

In the years following World War II older people in this country were seen as a huge societal problem. No group had been so ignored as older people were then. There was a period of time between the end of work and the end of life that former labor leader Walter Reuther aptly described as "too old to work, too young to die." People entering this age were lost. Too many didn't know what to do, and society didn't seem to want them. Age was viewed simply as the residue of youth.

But in the 1950s we saw the emergence of a life stage we think of today as "retirement." The plight of older people began to change. This was a time of tremendous demographic upheaval in the United States brought on by the birth of the baby boom generation. We created a social infrastructure to support and nurture this demographic disruption, woven together by private investment, public policy, and personal responsibility. The nation responded by investing in school construction, teacher education, housing, highways, and public health. The government created the Department of Health, Education, and Welfare and built the interstate highway system. The GI Bill made it possible for hundreds of thousands of returning soldiers to get an education and, thus, a good job. American families discovered a new place to live called suburbia. We invested in research and put America's best scientists and doctors to work developing vaccines and cures for childhood diseases. As a result, diseases such as polio, which afflicted thousands of children every year, have all but been eradicated. Vaccinations for chicken pox, measles, and mumps are now the rule and not the exception. Businesses flooded the market with new products and services geared toward children and families. At the same time, nonprofit organizations like AARP began to advocate for the rights of the elderly and advance a new philosophy of productive aging. As the concept of retirement began to take hold and these new demographic and cultural shifts took place, old age was being transformed from purgatory to a much desired destination.

It's no coincidence that we also began to see the dramatic rise of the middle class during this time. Business, government, private citizens, and organizations functioned under a social contract that saw America as a place where everyone had an opportunity to achieve the American Dream.

The benefits of this social contract were felt by people throughout society, including older Americans. The promise of Social Security was beginning to provide more and more people with a foundation for income in retirement. In 1965 we added Medicare, to ensure that older Americans would also have basic health care, and Medicaid, to protect and lift up the poor. And the number of Americans covered by guaranteed pensions rose steadily from 10.3 million in 1950 to 35 million in 1970. By 1980 28 percent of the workforce was covered by a defined-benefit pension plan.

Before long we began to see older adult living communities spring up with names like "Sun City" and "Leisure World." And what used to be thought of as old-age hell was being transformed into what became known as "The Golden Years." A retirement full of leisure became the reward for a life well spent—the cornerstone of the American Dream. Moreover, the sooner you got there, the better. To be able to retire was the ultimate symbol of success—and for many people, it still is.

We are now experiencing another demographic upheaval as the baby boomers age. Tens of millions of people in their fifties, sixties, seventies, and beyond are leading longer, healthier, more productive lives. They're beginning to wake up to this new longevity—and what it means in their lives— and in the process are creating a new life stage.

The Extended Middle Age

Today, despite what the birthday cards say, turning fifty no longer marks the beginning of a long, slow descent into old age; instead, it marks the beginning of a new period of growth, an extended middle age that did not exist for most of our ancestors. It's a time when people start embracing the idea of living longer, living better, and maintaining a balanced, vital lifestyle. This new life stage is still being defined. Some are calling it "The Third Chapter," "The Opportunity Generation," or "The Encore Stage." I simply call it extended middle age. It's now seen as a time when people have the freedom and opportunity to do things they've always wanted to do.

Those of us entering this period of our lives don't want to be defined by our age, and we don't want to live in fear that our possibilities become more limited as we get older. We believe our life experience has tremendous value. We still want to make a difference in the world. And because of increased longevity and generally better health, we still have a lot of years left to do it.

In September 2014 I had the opportunity to attend one of Oprah's "The Life You Want" sessions. As she stood on stage, inspiring the crowd with her rags-to-riches story, I couldn't help but see that through her life, she is perfectly embodying this hunger so many of us have to achieve more and greater things, no matter our age. I leaned over to my colleague and said, "Wow, she is still reaching for a deeper purpose." She has fame, fortune, and influence, but listening to her, I could still sense something was missing, that she still felt she had more to do, more to give. This new life stage gives us more time—in many cases thirty years more—to do and to give and to fulfill.

This extended middle age is much more than the residue of youth; it is a chance to grow in new and rewarding ways, to discover new roles, to redefine ourselves in ways that would have not been thought possible a few short years ago, to unleash our passions, to find and fulfill our purpose in life. We can live our best lives, achieving financial security, strength, health, meaningful work, romance, and discovery.

The Five New Realities of Aging

This all sounds great, right? Well, not quite. We must face the fact that it's not all sunshine, roses, and living the American Dream. Many people at this stage of life struggle to navigate economic, health, social, and technological realities unlike any generation before them. And many don't know where to turn for help or guidance. They find that many of society's institutions are stuck in a mindset designed for a twentieth-century life course. For example, many businesses are reluctant to recruit, retrain, and retain older workers. Colleges and universities are still trying to figure out how to attract older students who want to return to school. Our transportation systems are not designed to meet the needs of older people. Our houses were not built to accommodate our needs as we age. And many of our programs that assist people as they age were designed for a twentieth-century lifestyle and must be adapted to work better simply because people are aging differently today.

These disturbing trends bring into sharp focus many of the problems we face, highlighting the need to disrupt the system and rethink aging policies and practices in America. We not only have to help society adapt to the millions of people entering this new life stage; we have to help individuals as well. As we seek new solutions that give us more and better choices for living and aging, we, as individuals and as a society, have to face up to the new realities of aging.

Aging Is Really About Living

Once a month I have lunch with a group of girlfriends who range in age from their early fifties to mid-seventies. As we sit and chat about what's going on in our lives, it always occurs to me that no one passing by our table would ever guess these women's ages. They all look fabulous, dressed to the nines in stylish outfits that reflect their exuberance for life.

It seems like every conversation is about plans for the future—upcoming trips, home renovations, adventures. Of course, we also share stories of our struggles. But even those have a tone of optimism that illustrates their clear sense that experience has value. Each one of them owns her age, not trying to be, act, or look younger but simply trying to be the best lawyer, doctor, teacher, business owner, lobbyist, grandmother, caregiver, or homemaker she can be.

Everyone in the group understands the rigors of family caregiving and recognizes that they may need help in providing care for a loved one. They also wonder who will provide care if and when they need it. They love the idea of being up on the latest smartphone or tablet, even though they may need help figuring it out. They are aware that as they get older, they will become more of a target for a scam or for identity theft, and they want to know how to protect themselves. And they worry about increasing medical costs and how to meet them.

These women are realistic. When we are together, we dish out straight talk and help each other face what's next. We know our needs are changing, and although we may not always like it, we face it head on. We are open to change and find strength in each other as we ponder downsizing, retirement, and the unpredictable future.

My girlfriends and I share these outlooks and attitudes with millions of Americans our age. Like most people, we're busy living our lives, curious about what the future will bring and doing our best to make the most of it. We're involved with our families, our friends, the people in our communities. We don't stop and withdraw from society because we become a certain age. We understand that some aspects of life get a little tougher and some get a little easier as we get older, but it's all part of living, and we're determined to make the most of it. In short, we reflect the new reality of aging— it's all about living.

50 Million Shades of Gray—
Not Everyone Is Living Longer

Although we know that on the whole, people are living longer and better than ever before, we also know that great disparities exist among the people who comprise the fifty-and-over population. And though the US economy is the wealthiest in the world, quite a large part of our population lives in poverty, and there is a direct link between poverty and health and life expectancy. One of the new realities of aging is that we must understand and deal with the disparities that exist among our aging population.

How people age differs widely based on gender, race, and ethnicity. In 2010 white males reaching age sixty-five, on average, could expect to live to eighty-two. This is about three years less, on average, than white women, but two years longer than African American men. Black women, on average, do not live as long as white women.

Data from the Centers for Disease Control and Prevention show that Hispanics and blacks tend to be in poorer health than white non-Hispanics. They are less likely to exercise three days a week or more, suffer from higher rates of diabetes, are more likely to have a disability, and die at higher rates from various cancers. They are also more likely to suffer from cognitive impairment or Alzheimer's disease than are white non-Hispanics. This is largely because they have less access to adequate health insurance, less access to quality care, and a lower rate of health literacy. They also tend to have lower incomes, less in savings, and less in home equity than white non-Hispanics.

Gender, race, and ethnicity are not the only factors that influence longevity; affluence and education are also key factors. Men in the upper half of income distribution now live roughly 6 years longer than they did in the 1970s, whereas men in the lower half live just 1.3 years longer. Shockingly, white women without a high school diploma actually lost five years of life expectancy between 1990 and 2008.

Where you live is also a factor in determining how long you will live. Life expectancy is nearly seven years longer where I live, in northern Virginia, than it is where I work, in Washington, DC. In Cook County, Illinois (the Chicago area), there is a thirty-three-year difference in life expectancy depending upon where one lives within the county. Researchers are not clear why this discrepancy exists, but they expect that it may be due to higher levels of stress, obesity, and smoking that are more prevalent among society's have-nots, along with lower access to healthy foods and health care.

All of this matters because over the next forty years white non-Hispanics will continue to decline as a proportion of the US population. Today African Americans and Hispanics each represent over 10 percent of the over-fifty population, and Asians represent just over 4 percent. By 2030 racial and ethnic minorities will comprise 42 percent of the US population, and the Census Bureau projects that in 2044 Hispanics will surpass 25 percent of the population, making them America's largest racial/ethnic minority. This new demographic is creating what author Guy Garcia calls "The New Mainstream," where minorities make up the new majority, and the economic and cultural forces that are inherent within it will increasingly be a defining factor in the new reality of aging.

Older People Are Contributors, Not Burdens

Working in Washington, DC, I'm right at the heart of much of the misunderstanding about aging. Don't get me wrong: misperceptions and outdated stereotypes exist everywhere. But their impact is felt most strongly in Washington. It is a place steeped in the outdated view that getting older is about decline, that it presents only challenges, and that older people are a burden society has to contend with, a drain on our communal resources. We at AARP hear this all the time, especially when it comes to discussions about Social Security and Medicare. We hear things like: *The aging of the population will bankrupt the country. In twenty years the entire federal budget will be spent on programs for old people. We can't expect younger workers with families to pay higher taxes to support older retirees.* These attitudes ignore the new reality of aging: that it's about growth, not decline; that although it presents challenges, it also creates opportunities; and that older people are not burdens but contributors. We have to correct these misperceptions so we can develop new solutions to allow more people to choose how they want to live and age.

In his book *Boomer Nation*, historian Steve Gillon observed that, "At heart the boomers were consumers, not revolutionaries." As the boomer generation has moved into their fifty-and-over years—and as the first boomers turn seventy this year—they continue to be consumers. Along with their older brothers and sisters, they comprise a longevity economy that is disrupting conventional thinking and outdated stereotypes about aging's impact on the country and our economy as well as changing America both economically and socially.

The 106 million people age fifty and older who comprise the Longevity Economy account for over $7.1 trillion in annual economic activity. By 2032 that number is expected to rise to over $13.5 trillion. And here's a fact that may surprise you: the Longevity Economy is now larger than that of any country except the United States and China.

As people enter extended middle age, they contribute to the fabric of society socially as well as economically in their roles as volunteers, caregivers, and grandparents. Laura Carstensen, director of the Stanford Center on Longevity, says one of the true benefits of our increased longevity is having five to six generations living all at once. The impact of older generations with the ability to teach and influence younger ones is immeasurable.

I can't help but think what a wonderful blessing it is to have a growing number of older adults available to nurture and teach our young people today. It's true that families are more dispersed geographically; however, today we have Facebook, Skype, FaceTime, Twitter, Snapchat, and many other resources that help people stay connected.

People fifty and over love this technology. Half of all boomers are on Facebook, and women over fifty are the fastest growing segment of Facebook users. I know that when I get together with my family and friends, the first thing we do is get out our smartphones or tablets and show each other pictures of our kids, grandkids, nieces, and nephews and talk about what they are up to in their lives. And I'm sure many of you do the same thing. For some people, thinking of a grandparent brings to mind the image of a gray-haired little old lady with a child in her arms contently sitting in a rocking chair singing the baby to sleep. Although that makes for a lovely Norman Rockwell painting, the reality is much different today: the average age of a first-time grandparent in the United States is forty-eight, and grandparents do much more with their grandchildren than rock them in rocking chairs. They are paying for their college educations; buying them cars and clothing; and taking them to movies and restaurants and on vacations; and nearly 6 million grandchildren live with their grandparents. In 2009 grandparents spent nearly $52 billion as consumers (spoiling their grandchildren!).

Now, I ask you, when you read all of these numbers and consider all of these facts, can you really conclude that aging is only about decline? That aging presents only challenges? That older people are simply burdens? Frustratingly, a significant part of our government believes that addressing the needs of 106 million people who generate economic activity valued at $7.1 trillion is an unaffordable cost and a financial burden. But in the private sector more and more entrepreneurs are beginning to see the aging population as a great opportunity.

Aging Spurs Innovation

When we think of innovation we usually imagine some new product or service, an invention that revolutionizes our lives or that's never been done or seen before—the smartphone or the 3D printer or the driverless car, for example. Of course, these kinds of innovations have a huge impact on how we live our lives, but our quality of life in the future will also be determined by innovations in how products are designed, how services are delivered, and how policies are implemented. For example, the emerging sharing economy with companies like Uber, Airbnb, and TaskRabbit are changing the way we obtain services we need and teaching us that we don't necessarily have to own products in order to take advantage of the benefits they provide. We're changing the way health care is delivered and developing new vehicles for saving for and financing our future. In other words, when we think about new solutions that enable us to age on our own terms, we also have to think about social innovation.

In contrast to business innovation, which is often designed to address individual needs and interests, social innovation is more about finding new solutions to social needs or problems such as hunger, isolation, and affordable housing. It can take place within government, the for-profit sector, or the nonprofit sector, and it often involves collaboration among them. Social innovations can be new hybrids of existing products, services, and models rather than completely new, and they often cut across organizational or disciplinary boundaries and create compelling new relationships between previously separate individuals and groups. Social innovation helps change society as well as helps people live their best lives.

So what kinds of solutions are people seeking today, and what role does innovation, both business and social, play in creating those solutions? Considering what we know about the new reality of aging and the longevity economy, to say that innovation plays a key role is a gross understatement. Innovation is driving the new reality of aging and is the engine for disrupting aging—and technology is the driver of innovation.

Even though those of us over fifty are often perceived to be technophobic, we are the first adult tech-savvy generation. We grew up inspired by technology. From television to landing a man on the moon to computers to smartphones, this generation is more attuned than any before us to the power of technology to improve lives. We have come to expect technology to help us live longer and better. We demand products and services that meet our every need. We expect them to be faster and cheaper while providing even more capability. And as technology and social innovations evolve exponentially faster, we will seek out trusted guides to help us sort through the choices, information, and claims to help determine which products, services, and programs meet our specific needs. The companies and organizations that make our lives easier will benefit from our staggering numbers as customers and win in the marketplace.

For this generation of Americans fifty and older, the definition of the good life has shifted from owning a home, a nice car, and having a good job to place even more importance on good health, a financially secure future, and satisfying relationships. We are also transitioning from an era of wanting material things as a way of expressing who we are to searching for experiences that we find fulfilling and that make us happy. As such, we will continue to look for products, services, and programs that meet those needs and interests.

What's happening today is that we're beginning to see the merging of product and service solutions to meet the wants and needs of multiple life stages. People don't live their lives in silos, and they don't want siloed solutions. They're dealing with issues related to health, wealth, and self all at once. They're thinking about their futures—where they're going to live, how they're going to get around, how they're going to stay connected to their friends and family, how they're going to get health care and long-term care if they need it, how they're going make their money last. They're thinking about how to live a longer life in the best way possible.

We're beginning to see more and more technological innovations to bring "smart" technologies into the home to assist individuals in living independently longer in their own homes, monitoring and managing their daily activities, and keeping them connected to family and friends to avoid becoming isolated. We're also seeing more innovative uses of digital technology for self-care—wearables for monitoring and tracking vital signs, online communities for getting reactions to a doctor's recommendation before acting on it, healthcare navigators or care coordinators to help manage their health care, and electronic health records.

In addition, communities are developing comprehensive strategies to change their physical infrastructure and the way they deliver services, including housing and transportation services, to make their communities more livable and age-friendly.

Innovation is also finding its way into the personal fulfillment aspects of aging. We're seeing new products and services related to travel, wellness, personal relationships, entertainment and leisure, and the fun side of life. As we begin to see this life stage as a time of growth instead of decline, to identify the opportunities as well as the challenges and recognize older people as contributors instead of burdens, these innovations will likely introduce new ways of living across generations, affecting people across the life span.

But we're not talking about designing solutions just for old people. If people today think a product or service is designed for an old person, neither the young nor the old will buy it or use it. The new reality is that we are most drawn to innovations that help people of all ages live longer lives and improve the quality of life for everyone.

Our Perceptions of Aging Are Out of Sync with Reality

We can't underestimate how powerful the messages on those birthday cards are. They not only help define and perpetuate our perceptions of aging; they also create an expectation of how we are supposed to be, what we are supposed to do, and how we are supposed to see and treat other people. Disrupting aging requires us to reexamine our beliefs and attitudes about getting older. The convergence of longer life expectancy and technological advances is opening new doors to exploration and discovery as well as new expectations and new possibilities.

Yet while the aging landscape is changing more rapidly than ever before, our perceptions, as individuals and as a society, are simply out of sync with the new reality of aging. Most of us have an opportunity our ancestors never had. We have a "longevity bonus" of years—most of them spent in relatively good health—to pursue happiness, help others, serve our nation, give of ourselves to a cause or a purpose that we believe in, and lead positive social change that will make our country—and our world—better for all our citizens. It's a great gift, a tremendous opportunity we ought not to waste. Why do we insist on perpetuating stereotypes that will affect each and every one of us someday?

What Does It All Mean?

The increased longevity of our population has been called "the true wealth of nations." And the new reality of aging challenges each of us to recognize that our potential is not depleted with age any more than it is limited by youth. It is something we can look forward to as an exciting new phase of our lives. But we cannot leave our future to kismet. We must take responsibility for our futures, planning and preparing for the transitions along the way.

Aging is a certainty. It affects everyone, not just on an individual level but in our society as well. We must work to adapt our social structures, institutions, and public policies and programs to meet the challenges and take advantage of the opportunities an aging society creates.

At the same time, we also need to re-imagine our own lives in order to better navigate life's transitions, find meaning and purpose, and get the most out of life in this vastly changing world.

The new reality of aging forces us to see that even though the way people are aging is changing, the solutions available to us as we age are out of sync with how we want to live. Why? Because many of them are based on outdated beliefs and attitudes that still reflect old, negative stereotypes of aging.

Disrupting aging is not just about re-imagining old age; it's about designing our lives and creating social institutions, public policies, and personal behaviors that support us. Young people today are setting out on a life course that is as different from ours as ours was from our parents'. There is a high probability that many will live well past one hundred in relatively good health. That's the new reality of aging. It's not a concept or a theory—it's here. We must plan for it, prepare for it, and make the most of it. And it all begins with each one of us choosing to become comfortable with the fact that we are getting older and that all those well-intentioned birthday cards are simply wrong. We are not over the hill. We are owning our age, and it's going to be awesome.

CHAPTER 2

Own Your Age

I've enjoyed every age I've been, and each has had its own individual merit. Every laugh line, every scar, is a badge I wear to show I've been present, the inner rings of my personal tree trunk that I display proudly for all to see. Nowadays, I don't want a "perfect" face and body; I want to wear the life I've lived.

—PAT BENATAR

Did you ever stop to think how old you would be if you didn't know how old you are? It's an intriguing question. How does knowing your age affect the way you behave, what you do, and what you don't do? How often do we give in to society's— or the media's—idea of what "old" is? What if we could rid ourselves of this preoccupation with age?

What if we focused more on the day-to-day act of *living*? Would we behave any differently? Would we treat other people any differently? Would we be happier and enjoy life more?

For Hall of Fame pitcher Leroy "Satchel" Paige, that question was more than hypothetical. Paige joined the Cleveland Indians in 1948 and helped lead them to the American League pennant that year. It was his first year in the majors—having spent the past twenty years in the Negro Leagues—and he was the oldest major league rookie that year, by a lot. We now know that he was forty-two when he joined the Indians, but at that time, he didn't. He'd never seen his birth certificate, but it never really seemed to bother him. Today it's hard to find baseball players over the age of forty, and playing past fifty is unheard of—but Satchel Paige was different, in more ways than one.

Reporters would constantly ask him, "How can you play at your age? What keeps you going?" He would simply say that because he didn't know how old he was, he was never held back from performing the way he knew he could.

"Age is a question of mind over matter," he would say. "If you don't mind, it doesn't matter."

Well, for better or for worse (probably worse), most of us do know how old we are. And unlike Satchel Paige, we do allow our perceptions of age to influence how we behave. But wouldn't it be great if we never knew our actual age? Then age wouldn't hold us back either. How freeing that would be.

If you're like me, you just want to do what you want to do, when you want to do it. In fact, that's how most of us aspire to live as we get older, but we often don't because we can't get past the perception that we are entering a time of deterioration, dependency, and decline, an idea that unfortunately has been drilled into us all of our lives. So we go one of two ways: either we just accept it and slip quietly into our later years, or we go into denial, fighting it with every fiber of our being—and in some cases with every dollar in our bank account. As a result, "aging as decline" becomes a self-fulfilling prophecy. It's true that many of us define ourselves by our jobs. So when we retire, we often unthinkingly describe ourselves in the past tense: "I used to be a teacher," or "I used to be a nurse," or "I used to work at Chevrolet." How sad! If you see yourself as an "I used to be . . . ," how do you expect the rest of society to see you?

So we are faced with a challenge. We have to change the outdated stereotypes and perceptions in our culture and society, and it starts with you. The first step is to look in the mirror and really ask yourself whether you need to "own your age." I'm not talking about just accepting it; I mean really own it, embrace it, feel good about where you are in life and, more importantly, about where you are going. If we can all do this, we will get to the point where we're no longer defined by the outdated expectations of what we should or should not do at a certain age and create more solutions that allow us to choose the way we want to live as we get older.

Aging is not a problem any more than living is—it's a human experience, a natural part of life. If you think about it, many of the issues we face as we grow older have very little to do with age or youth. They evolve around life's experiences, and our life experiences at fifty or sixty or seventy are much different from what they are at twenty or thirty or forty. And that's the way it should be. Experience matters. It has value and helps define who we are and the contributions we make to society at any age. Mohammed Ali once said that people who see life the same way at fifty as they did at twenty have wasted thirty years of their lives. In today's world we might add that people who see life at eighty the same way they did at fifty have also wasted thirty years.

I won't pretend that the aging process doesn't affect us—it does. But it's time we put aging in the proper perspective. We're all moving along life's continuum. We can't go back or stay where we are even if we wanted to—and most of us don't want to. But we can't allow society—whether it be the media, advertisers, or popular culture—to delude us into thinking we can or should want to stay young. That leads to a sense of self-denial about who we are and where we are in life as well as, ultimately, a feeling of despair and hopelessness.

If staying "forever young," as the song says, is our goal in life, we will never achieve it, no matter how many plastic surgeries we have, how much moisturizer we buy, age-defying makeup we use, or vitamin supplements we take. Staying vital, on the other hand, is something we can all achieve. In fact, more and more of us are achieving it every day. Take tennis great Martina Navratilova. Today, at age fifty-nine, she is as physically fit and mentally tough as she was during her playing days. I recall, while at a fundraising event with her in Dallas, she was conducting a private tennis camp for some of our donors. I was hitting the ball and she was giving me a few tips. I told her I used to be very athletic. She replied, "I can tell you used to be." Now, if that isn't enough to make you want to get back in shape, I don't know what is. Martina isn't a *used to be*; she is as vital today as ever. A compelling advocate for personal fitness and healthy living, Martina travels the world speaking at events, writing, and tirelessly motivating thousands of people to live healthier lifestyles by taking simple steps to a better life. Though she no longer competes on the professional tennis circuit, she loves to play exhibition matches. After all, she says, "The ball doesn't know how old I am."

Fight Ageism, Not Age

I have to admit: I never really thought much about my age until I went to work at AARP. I never really saw it as a defining factor in my life or thought about how it influenced what I could or could not do. But when I saw how age had either accelerated or held others back through subtle forms of discrimination or through blatant, in-your-face discrimination, this turned into something I couldn't ignore. The first time I can remember experiencing age discrimination was when I was in my twenties. I was applying for a position with the federal government. My recommendations were good enough to get me an interview for the job, but when I went in, the interviewer looked at me and said, "I thought you were older. I think you're a bit too young for this job." (Translation: "There's no way I'm going to hire you.") Because of my age, I remember thinking, *his loss.*

We are a society obsessed with age. I've always thought comedian Larry Miller described it best:

Do you realize that the only time in our lives when we like to get old is when we're kids? If you're less than ten years old, you're so excited about aging that you think in fractions.

"How old are you?"

"Four . . . and a half!"

You're never thirty-six and a half.

AND . . . goin' on five. See, that's the key there: "Going on!" You're so excited about getting older, you're . . . Goin' on!

You get into your teens, and now you're so thrilled you jump whole numbers.

"How old are you?"

"I'm gonna be sixteen." I'm twelve, but I'm going to be sixteen!

Then the highlight of the experience: you become twenty-one.

See, even the word "become" sounds wonderful. It's theatrical, it's magical! You BECOME . . . twenty-one!

But that's as good as it gets. It all changes after that. You're four-and-a-half, yes, you're going to be sixteen, sure, you become twenty-one, okay, but then you . . .

TURN . . . thirty.

Whoa. What happened there? "Turn?" It makes you sound like bad milk.

He TURNED thirty—we had to throw him out.

Not so much fun anymore, is it? Now it gets ugly. You become twenty-one, you turn thirty . . .

Then, you're PUSHING forty.

Stay over there, forty. I'm pushing you back.

But it doesn't stop there. You BECOME twenty-one; you TURN thirty; you're PUSHING forty;

And you REACH . . . fifty!

"Oh, my dreams are gone . . ."

But now it's going too fast. You become twenty-one, you turn thirty, you're pushing forty, you reach fifty . . .

And you HIT sixty. I can't stop, I can't stop!

You become twenty-one, you turn thirty, you're pushing forty, you reach fifty, you hit sixty . . .

And you MAKE IT . . . to seventy. "I didn't think I was going to make it."

After that it's day by day.

You become . . . tired. You turn . . . four-thirty.

My grandmother won't even buy green bananas.

Into your nineties you start going backward. "I was JUST
. . . ninety-two.

But a strange thing happens, folks. If you can make it over
one hundred, you become a little kid again.

"I'm a hundred and four . . . AND A HALF!"

We laugh because what Larry Miller was talking about
is so familiar to all of us. It's ingrained in our culture, and
we've all experienced it with our own families. But what his
rant also illustrates is how deeply ageism is entrenched in
our language. We hear its echo reverberate through our language every day.

"Are you having a senior moment?"

"Isn't that dress a bit young for you?"

"You're going to have a hard time finding a job at your age."

"Are you sure you can remember all that? Should I write it
down for you?"

We not only live in an aging society; we live in an ageist
society. It's not our own aging we need to fight against but
the ageist attitudes and perceptions that permeate our society and play such a huge role in shaping our culture. What
makes ageist attitudes and practices so difficult to change
is that many people are not even aware they practice ageism. So we have to change the mindset and build an awareness of ageism to set the foundation for changing the social
norms. We all have a responsibility—young and old—to
speak out against ageism, to become aware of how our ageist attitudes and perceptions work their way into our behaviors and our language and to stop making jokes that subtly

and unintentionally promote ageism. It's one thing to have a sense of humor about our own aging but quite another to believe the myths and stereotypes—and, worse yet, to start living them. Today it is socially unacceptable to ignore, ridicule, or stereotype someone based on their gender, race, or sexual orientation. So why is it still acceptable to do this to people based on their age?

Perhaps the bigger question is: Why does this matter? It matters primarily for two reasons. First, ageism—and the negative perception of aging that it perpetuates—creates a negative reality of aging. And as long as that exists, we will never face up to the changes we need to make to adapt to our aging society. Second, it's bad enough that ageism can influence public policy, employment practices, and how people are treated in society, but what's worse is that we accept the ageist behavior ourselves and start acting it out. The result is that we limit our own choices about how we age.

Have you ever complained about an ache or a pain in your knee or hip only to hear someone say, "Well, you're not as young as you used to be. You've got to expect these little aches and pains as you get older." Then, you think to yourself, *Yeah, I guess she's right, I am getting older.* That can make you feel even worse than the pain you're having.

What if, instead, you thought, *My other knee is the same age, and it doesn't hurt. Maybe something else besides my age is causing the pain.* It may not help the pain in your knee, but I'll bet you would feel better. And I bet you would do something about that pain in your knee rather than just accepting it as a consequence of getting older.

Actress and singer Rita Moreno is a great example for us all of someone admirably flying in the face of the ageist stereotypes that surround us. Rita has been performing for six decades and is one of only twelve people—and the first—to win an Oscar, an Emmy, a Tony, and a Grammy. "Growing old in Hollywood is a serious deficit," she said. "I had battled racism and sexism all my life. Now I had to battle ageism. But, I refused to compromise and make myself look younger than my age." At eighty-four, she is still performing, has just released a new album, and loves spending time with her grandchildren. Rita Moreno owns her age, and as a result, she is living the life she wants to live as she gets older.

Harvard psychologist Ellen Langer offers another perspective on this in her book, *Counterclockwise*. She notes that if an older person has difficulty getting in and out of a car, we often assume they have weak legs or a bad sense of balance rather than considering the inadequacies of a seat that doesn't swivel and allow the passenger to emerge straight ahead rather than sideways out of a car. Wouldn't that make it easier for all of us? If a twenty-five-year-old had difficulty riding a tricycle, would we assume it was due to an enlargement of her limbs or a loss of flexibility? Nope.

Tricycles were not made with twenty-five-year-olds in mind, and car seats were not made with seventy-five-year-olds in mind. But we'll get to that more in a later chapter. The point is that every day, older people are forced to navigate an environment that was designed neither by nor for them. We often blame our limitations on the fact that we're getting older. But in reality it may simply be that our environment doesn't fit us anymore or that the product isn't designed to fit our needs.

Once we muster the courage to admit that and do something about it—like adapting the car seat to meet the needs of the seventy-five-year-old instead of blaming the person—we can begin to develop creative solutions that benefit people of all ages.

Last year at our Life@50+ National Event & Expo in Miami, I appeared in front of the more than six thousand AARP members. I was there to advocate for owning your age. To make my point, I wore a button that said, "Fearless at 57!" After the speech we had buttons available for people to pick up that they could write their age on and wear. I was overwhelmed by the number of people I saw at the event proudly wearing their buttons displaying their age. People came up to me to tell me how freeing it felt to show their age. As one sixty-eight-year-old woman told me, "It's so liberating!" Another woman, seventy-four years old, told me, "No one's going to deprive me of my age—I've earned every day of it."

That's disrupting aging. That's what happens when we own our age. Oh, and remember that interviewer who told me when I was twenty-two that I was too young to be hired? He called back two weeks later and offered me the job and kicked off my career. The rest is history!

What Is It About Turning Fifty?

Of all the things I do as CEO of AARP, I'm probably most well known for—or, some would say, despised for—sending that letter. You know the one. It's the one you get when you turn fifty, inviting you to become members of AARP. Apparently not everyone is thrilled to receive "the letter." Some people just throw it in the trash without ever opening it. Some sneaky spouses intercept it in the mail, open it, frame it, and present it to their husbands or wives in front of all their friends at their fiftieth birthday party as a joke or repurpose it as a birthday card (but we've already covered that topic, and you would never do that, right?). In 1998 humorist Bill Geist devoted a whole chapter to the letter in his book *The Big Five-Oh!: Facing, Fearing, and Fighting Fifty*, in which he referred to AARP's chief executive at that time as "the evil Horace Deets." He said that because there was no longer a draft for military service and the Unabomber had been captured, the most feared piece of mail you could receive was a letter from Horace. Don't get me wrong: a lot of people welcome my invitation and sign up—some 38 million, in fact— but some just can't face the fact that they're turning fifty.

So what is it about turning fifty that causes such a visceral reaction? If you type into Google, "I lie about my . . ." the first word that pops up is "age." Why do they hate getting older so much? And why does it all seem to begin at age fifty instead of, say, sixty-five or seventy or eighty? The answer, of course, is long-outdated cultural stereotypes. We're conditioned. Nothing biological happens to you on your fiftieth birthday to suddenly make you old. And nothing biological happens to you on your sixty-fifth birthday that makes you want to retire and move to the sunbelt or move in with your kids (hi, kids!). Aging is a gradual, continuous process. It begins the day we are born and continues until the day we die.

When we are younger, we see aging as a process of growth and development. We're learning and maturing and becoming productive members of society who use our talents and skills to contribute to the overall good of society. We have constant reminders—or markers—of our growth and development. We start school at five, we're promoted every year, we are confirmed in the church or bar mitzvahed or bah mitzvahed at thirteen, we can get our driver's license at sixteen, we graduate high school and become young adults at eighteen, and we become twenty-one with all the rights and privileges of adulthood that this entails. Each milestone is marked with a celebration or a reward noting our achievement for reaching yet another growth point in our lives.

Then for some reason, when we hit middle age, around fifty or so, we start to think of aging as a process of decline and deterioration. It's like we've reached the top of the mountain, and now we're on our way down—hence the phrase, "over the hill." And as we all know, you go downhill a lot faster than you go up, so we get it into our minds that the decline is happening faster. Now, if this were the 1930s, when average life expectancy was about sixty-two, I could understand this line of thinking. I wouldn't necessarily agree with it, but I could understand why people would think that way. But today, when people turning fifty can expect to live another thirty-plus years, it makes no sense.

For the most part the markers disappear as we get older. They're certainly fewer and farther between. And those that do exist are not met so much with celebration as they are with dread. It's not that we don't have milestones to celebrate as we get older; it's just that we don't recognize them with such a spirit of celebration and joy. And what a shame that is.

Another reason fifty is such a big deal for many of us is that it becomes a time of reflection. We begin to "take stock": What goals have I accomplished, and what's left still to do? Have I lived the life I set out to live when I was twenty? Am I happy? What's next for me?

How we answer these questions often stirs up a wide range of emotions and determines how we view our lives as we get older. One of my friends who by all accounts has led an incredibly successful life is now faced with the fact that she is aging. Her children are gone, living their own lives, and she is struggling to find meaning and purpose in her own life. She is stuck in the "aging as decline" mindset and can't see the opportunities for growth and joy and happiness in front of her. My friends and I try to encourage her to own her age, to feel good about her accomplishments, and to realize that she has choices in how to spend the next twenty years of her life. We tell her that success and joy are not just for the young but can be accomplished at any age. But she is not alone; it's a struggle for many people.

Many people are already beginning to realize this. Take, for example, Ernestine Shepherd. With her flat stomach, toned arms, and excellent health, you'd never guess this female bodybuilder is seventy-nine years old. Ms. Shepherd is in better shape than most people who are decades younger. Her personal mantra is to remain "determined, dedicated and disciplined to be fit." She says and clearly demonstrates that age is really nothing but a number. As impressive as her physique is, one of the most incredible parts of Shepherd's story is that she didn't even start working out until she was fifty-six. After overcoming many health problems, including depression, following the death of her sister, Shepherd set a goal to get in shape. She was declared the World's Oldest Performing Female Bodybuilder by the Guinness Book of World Records in 2010.

And then there is ninety-nine-year-old Doreetha Daniels. She became the oldest graduate ever at the College of the

Canyons in Santa Clarita, California, with an associate degree in social sciences. She just graduated in June 2015. Daniels said she wanted to finish her education to better herself. Her journey, which started in spring 2009, was wrought with personal difficulties. Seemingly routine tasks, such as driving to school and getting around the campus, were more difficult for her than for most of her fellow students, who were mostly eighteen to twenty-four years old. In the classroom other challenges presented themselves, namely her need to master the computer in order to complete modern college courses. She also experienced issues related to hearing class lectures and keeping pace with other students. But she persevered: "It's been sixty-three years since I've taken algebra even," said Daniels at the time. "But I've learned a lot."

Recognizing these challenges, Daniels just worked harder. And eventually that work paid off. Twice a week she would spend time in the campus Tutoring and Learning Center doing homework and working with tutors—all before class even started.

Her desire to get out of bed each day and go to school and face the challenges inside and outside of the classroom was an inspiration to everyone around her. Ms. Daniels advised prospective students: "Don't give up. Do it. Don't let anybody discourage you. Say that, 'I'm going to do it,' and do it for yourself."

Grammy Award–winning singer Regina Belle has a similar story. Last spring she completed a journey she started over thirty years ago, by returning to Rutgers University to complete her bachelor's degree. She said that earning her degree was just as meaningful as winning her Grammy. It was just something she had to do for herself.

Ernestine, Doreetha, and Regina are all owning their age. They all took stock of their lives and decided that they still had things they wanted to do for themselves. They knew that they could continue to grow and develop, and that's just what they did. They demonstrate that aging is not something to fear but something to look forward to, that it's not a period of decline but a period of growth. They also show us that if we are going to continue to grow and develop as we get older, we can't live in fear of aging; we have to be fearless at whatever age we are. We have to be willing to get out of our comfort zones, try new things, take chances, and defy the old stereotypes and misperceptions about what we should or should not do at a certain age.

So when you hit that scary number—whatever it is for you—just remind yourself that the journey is far from over. Just imagine all the years ahead of you that you can use to correct all the things you did wrong or wanted a second chance to get right. Just imagine you can now finally take that course you wanted to take in college but could never fit in or to learn to do something you always wanted to do. Those are the opportunities we have before us if we rid ourselves of the old mindset and own our age.

"Act Your Age"?

When I was growing up it seemed like my parents were always telling me, "Jo Ann, act your age." Now, as a parent, my kids are telling me, "Mom, act your age!" What does that mean? Just how am I supposed to act at fifty or sixty or at seventy or eighty or even one hundred? When you are a young mother, there are any number of books that tell you what to expect and what to do as your kids reach certain ages: *What to Expect When You're Expecting, What to Expect in the First Year, What to Expect from Toddlers,* and so on. But to my knowledge, no one has published a book advising you what to do when you're fifty or sixty-five or eighty—until now!

So we should ask ourselves: Was Ernestine Shepherd acting her age when she became a world-class body builder at the age of seventy-eight? Was Doreetha Daniels acting her age when she graduated from college at age ninety-nine? Was Regina Belle acting her age when she completed her thirty-year journey to a bachelor's degree at age fifty-one? Ten years ago we might have said no; they are the exceptions to the rule. But today we can say of course they are. They are no longer the exceptions to the rule; they are the rule.

Acting your age is based purely on the expectation of what we believe someone should or should not be able to do at a certain age. And those expectations are built to a great extent on what we perceive as old. Interestingly but not surprisingly, those perceptions change with age. As we get older we push the age at which we consider people to be "old" out farther. One survey found that adults under thirty believe the average person becomes old at age sixty. Middle-aged adults thought the average person becomes old at about seventy, and people over sixty-five said the average person doesn't become old until turning seventy-four. With the first of the boomers turning seventy this year, that number is bound to go up.

So ask yourself this question: If you believe fifty is the beginning of the end, and you're old at sixty-five, even though that's now considered middle age, how will you act your age at fifty or sixty-five? Or how will you act at eighty-five or ninety, and what will you do to act your age for the twenty to thirty years in between? If you believe that you can't teach an old dog new tricks (which isn't even true for dogs), does that mean you stop learning when you think you've become an old dog? And at what age does that occur? If you believe that older people have nothing to look forward to, nothing to contribute, and are a burden on society, how are you going to act your age when you're older?

It's not only a question of how we are going to act our age as individuals but also of how society is going to act. To adapt our public policies and social structures based on an outdated perception of aging mired in old myths and stereotypes would be one of the greatest social blunders in our nation's history. But if we think older people are all alike, with the same behaviors, needs, concerns, and desires, why would we need to offer choices in housing, transportation, health care, and so forth? If we think older people have nothing to contribute and are a burden on society, why would we need to look for ways for older people to continue to contribute to society? And wouldn't many of our programs that are designed to help people lead independent lives as they get older look much different?

Owning our age opens up new possibilities for leading more purposeful and fulfilling lives as we get older. It makes us realize that aging doesn't have to be one of life's great contradictions; we can live to a ripe old age without the fear of growing older. We can discover the real possibilities life has to offer. It also provides our society with new opportunities to take advantage of a large cohort of people fifty and older who comprise a reservoir of untapped wisdom, talent, and experience to solve our nation's problems and make this world a better place. And it makes it possible to build a society where people are valued because of who they are, not judged by how old they are.

If I could succeed in changing only one perception of aging, it would be for people to reach the milestone of their fiftieth birthday and say, "YES! I finally made it! Now I can finally join AARP. I've earned it!" When we reach that point and your children and grandchildren tell you to act your age at fifty, sixty-five, eighty-five, or one hundred, it will take on a whole new meaning.

CHAPTER 3

Design Your Life

The only worthy goal is to make a meaningful life
out of an ordinary one.
—PETER DRUCKER

When we're kids the question almost every adult asks us at some point is, "What do you want to be when you grow up?" Typically we answer with something like a doctor, a lawyer, a teacher, a fireman, or a ballerina. Once, when I asked a friend's granddaughter what she wanted to be when she grows up, she said, "I want to be famous." When I reflect back on what I wanted to be when I grew up, I think I had on my list a news anchor, but my father thought for sure I'd be a seamstress; he wasn't particularly fond of the fact that I might move out to go to college. And I was a very good seamstress. I still have the Singer sewing machine my parents bought me when I graduated from high school.

So we go about the business of planning our lives. We go to school to get our degree or the training we need, we get our first job, maybe meet our partner and start a family, and if all goes well, we have a nice long career. And then we reach the point—whether it's a certain age we've got in mind or our friends and colleagues are starting to reach it—when we think it must be time to slow down and settle into a well-deserved life of leisure. Then something unexpected happens: we realize we aren't ready to slip off into a quiet life. Not only do we still have plenty of years left to live; we also have plenty of life left to enjoy.

The problem is that many of us haven't planned for this part of our lives, and because we are living so much longer than previous generations, there aren't many role models to show us the way. We may have saved some money for our later years (though most people have not saved nearly enough), but how many of us actually have a plan in place for what we want to do in our extended middle age?

This is what I call "mindless aging." One day we discover our careers are winding down, our kids are grown, and we have another twenty-five or thirty years ahead of us without a clear idea of how to fill them. Our lives are not like those of our parents, and the assumptions we made about this part of our lives are no longer relevant. This is a time to shift from "mindless aging" to "mindful living." We begin to ask ourselves: "What's next in our lives?"

- What's next for parents who have raised their families and now find themselves empty nesters?
- What's next for those leaving long-held jobs after reaching retirement age?

- What's next for long-married people who find themselves newly single?
- What's next for parents who are in the midst of rearing their children and find they must now also care for their aging parents?
- What's next for people who just want to do something else but don't know what or how to go about finding what is right for them at this point in their lives?
- What's next for our society when for fifty years America has considered traditional retirement the ultimate destination, and now it isn't the only option or even the best option—and for many, it's no option at all?

As we contemplate how to answer these "What's next?" questions, we also begin to question not only what we are doing but also who we are. My bet is that many of us will begin to realize that the goals we set for ourselves in our youth were really about what we were going to do, not about who we are or the kind of person we want to be. I've been extremely fortunate to be able to work at places where I feel like I'm doing my best work and enjoying it far more than I ever imagined. But many of us reach a level of success in our careers only to find that our success hasn't brought us the happiness we seek; we want more out of life and start searching for other ways to find it.

This was what happened to Arianna Huffington. When I first met Arianna at AARPs Life@50+ National Event & Expo in 2014, she told me she could be the poster child for disrupting aging. After a successful career as an author and commentator, she started the *Huffington Post* in 2005 at the age of fifty-five. Even though she didn't know that much about technology at the time, she knew that the Internet was the best way to get out messages about important issues. So she learned the technology, surrounded herself with people who were good at it, and launched what the *Observer* would call in 2008 "the most powerful blog in the world."

She had reached the pinnacle of fame and success. *Time* magazine named her one of the world's 100 Most Influential People, and *Forbes* listed her as one of the World's 100 Most Powerful Women. She appeared on magazine covers and television programs, and her business was going gangbusters. In 2011 she sold the site to AOL for more than $300 million and became president and editor-in-chief of the company's Huffington Post Media Group.

Though it sounds so easy, it wasn't. In 2007, shortly after getting *Huffington Post* up and running, she collapsed from exhaustion and lack of sleep. This was her wake-up call. She began to question how she defined success. The eighteen-hour days she had been working brought her fame, fortune, and power, but it wasn't the life she wanted to live; it didn't bring her the fulfillment she was seeking. She realized that in order to live the kind of life she truly wanted to live, she had to redefine her notion of success. That set her on a journey to discover what it meant to lead the good life. She concluded that success wasn't defined just by money and power but also included *well-being,* taking care of ourselves; *wisdom,* that knowledge and judgment gained by the experience of living; *wonder,* our sense of delight in the mysteries of the universe and the everyday occurrences and small miracles that fill our lives; and *giving,* the willingness to give of ourselves prompted by our empathy and compassion for others. Her book, *Thrive,* details how she has put these principles to work in her own life, and it has served as an inspiration to me. When she spoke to the graduating class at Smith College in 2013 her message was not about how to climb the ladder of success but about redefining the meaning of success and what it means to live the good life.

The Midlife Quest

Arianna is not alone in her search for a more fulfilling life. Millions of us reach a point in our lives, usually somewhere between age forty and sixty, when we begin to realize our own mortality and begin to question the meaning of our lives and whether our success has brought us happiness. We even have a name for this: a "midlife crisis."

Professor and writer Joseph Campbell aptly described a midlife crisis as "what happens when you climb to the top of the ladder and discover it's against the wrong wall." This is a time when many of us reassess our achievements in terms of our dreams. We go through a period of re-evaluation and reflection, taking stock of where we are in life and where we're going, of who we are and who we want to be. Have we realized our goals? If not, what do we have to do to reach them? If we have achieved them, has that success given us the happiness and fulfillment we expected? If so, then what's next in our lives? If not, what do we need to do to find happiness and fulfillment? What is our purpose in life? What are we here for? How we answer these questions is the first step in the process of making significant changes in our careers, work-life balance, marriages, relationships, finances, and health.

It's also a time of transition—perhaps one of our most significant—when our children leave home or they move back,
we become caregivers for our parents, we become grandparents, we change jobs or careers, our appearance and physical health change, and we find ourselves free for perhaps the
first time in our adult lives to pursue lifelong dreams.

This can be an exciting but challenging time. And for
some there is an instinct to regain their youth, to look to
a time they remember as being happy and carefree rather
than approaching head on a life they may not have planned
for and is full of uncertainty.

So let's make a deal, shall we? Let's stop thinking of this
time as our "midlife crisis." It's really the beginning of a
journey—a midlife quest for happiness and fulfillment. It's
a matter of perspective, and if we avoid facing the future,
we won't gain all of the wonderful benefits that come to us
during this period of our lives. If we've been mindlessly aging for forty or fifty years, it's easy to get stuck in the aging as
decline mindset (it's no wonder we experience this period of
our lives as a midlife crisis). But if we begin living and aging
mindfully, we can begin to see aging as growth and discover
new opportunities for continued development.

My sister Diane is the perfect example. I don't know
whether she'd label it a midlife crisis, but she went through
something like this after her kids were grown. I don't think
I've ever known anyone who wanted more to be a mother—
and now a grandmother—than my sister Diane. And to say
she's good at it is an understatement. As far back as I can
remember Diane has devoted her whole life to her husband of forty-eight years and her two children. But once
the children were grown, out of college, and married and

my brother-in-law continued his work and extensive travel schedule, Diane found herself in search of something more.

Little did we know that Diane would soon discover her new passion just outside of Montego Bay, Jamaica. She virtually adopted Mt. Zion Primary School in St. James, Jamaica, a rural and remote Jamaican farming village literally just up the hill from the massive luxurious resorts lining Jamaica's north shore. Mt. Zion seems a world away—in fact, a third world away. Mt. Zion is often used to describe "the ultimate paradise," but this poverty-ridden farming village of about four hundred is anything but. When she started, about forty-two kids from kindergarten through sixth grade attended Mt. Zion Primary School.

From the moment Diane arrived at the one-room school, it was obvious that both the school building and the students were in need of a lot of help. The physical plant at the school was beaten down from years of neglect, and the literacy rate among the students in kindergarten through sixth grade was a dismal 40 percent.

So she went to work. Diane and, now, all of us—her family, friends and associates—participate in making life better for the children who attend the school. Diane and I are both members of The Links, Inc., the nation's largest women's volunteer service organization working in communities to enhance the lives of African Americans and other persons of African ancestry, and over the years we have involved several Link Chapters in our efforts. Today Link Chapters from across the country provide varying levels of material and financial support to Mt. Zion Primary School. This includes material items such as clothes and shoes, household goods such as towels, first aid supplies, and school supplies and library books. In addition, individuals helped to under-write the cost of a cook's salary, purchased a refrigerator and freezer, refurbished the bathroom, and built walls within the small school house.

Under Diane's leadership and direction we now fund feeding programs, school uniforms, tutoring, music and physical education programs and much more. Thanks to the work and support of volunteers, the school has improved the physical plant, hired a cook who makes nutritional meals for the students, and received a gift of musical instruments and monies to pay a music instructor. We also spearheaded a book drive to replace the meager collection of outdated li-brary books with exciting, new age–centric books for chil-dren of all ages as well as adults. The school now also has a community garden where the students are learning how to grow vegetables and fruits. Doctors and dentists have do-nated services and supplies to improve personal hygiene, and we have enticed various organizations and individuals to donate other much needed items as well.

But the most exciting progress has come in the classroom. The literacy rate at the school has jumped from 40 percent to 62 percent in 2012 and then to 100 percent in 2013, 2014, and 2015. This is a tremendous achievement that very few schools in the Montego Bay area ever achieve. And it means that the children of this school are now on their way to a bet-ter life and a brighter future.

The change in the children's lives are remarkable, but the happiness and fulfillment it has brought my sister are be-yond words. She has truly found her passion, her purpose for living, and that, along with her grandkids, is all she has ever wanted.

The Pursuit of Happiness

When Thomas Jefferson wrote in the Declaration of Independence that one of our unalienable rights is the pursuit of happiness, he wasn't using the phrase the way we might today. It didn't mean a pursuit of pleasure or entertainment; he was referring to pursuing the good life. He meant developing our individual talents and skills to our fullest potential to do good work. Happiness, to Jefferson, was achieved by contributing to the greater social good as a productive member of a community. I find myself in total agreement with Mr. Jefferson on that point. The best life includes contributing to the well-being of others, and we achieve happiness by fulfilling our purpose in life to the best of our abilities.

The late Dr. Gene Cohen, a world-renowned psychiatrist and expert on creativity and aging, brilliantly observed that age offers countless opportunities for growth, development, and creativity. This kind of growth can't be forced; it has to unfold in its own time. Just as you can't teach a child to read until her brain is developed, there are certain qualities of adulthood that emerge after we have lived much of our lives. It's generally referred to as wisdom, and it develops as a result of our age, as we gain intelligence, knowledge, emotional growth, and life experiences. Combined, all of these foster in us an ability to respond to complex situations, make it easier for us to define problems, project possible outcomes of our actions, approach new situations with confidence, and develop strategies for coping with life's ups and downs.

Dr. Cohen pointed out that many of the common and shared emotions we experience as we get older—those questions we ask ourselves as we take stock of our lives, for example—are natural development markers indicating our human potential. They are shaped by our chronological age, our history, and our circumstances, and they are characterized by how we view and experience life psychologically, emotionally, and intellectually. If we recognize them as such instead of as some terrible crisis to be reckoned with, we can make changes in our lives that allow us to continue to grow and develop, just as we did when we were children learning to read, ride a bike, or drive a car.

Have you ever said to yourself, *If I only knew then what I know now . . . ?* We do know now what we didn't know then, so why look backward? Why can't many of us see midlife as a time to pursue happiness instead of a time of crisis? One of the reasons is that at middle age and older, our culture has taught us to view the passage of time as a loss instead of an asset. As Cohen pointed out, development and growth often requires the passage of time. We can't effectively take stock of our lives and decide whether we have succeeded until we've had experiences worth assessing. We can't experience the freedom that comes with age without first having spent considerable time being tied down by commitments and competing priorities. Although we can search for meaning and purpose throughout our lives at any age, it becomes more relevant and important to us in later life because it's based on decades of life experiences.

One of the great benefits of an extended middle age is that it gives us more freedom and time to pursue happiness. Often freed from the responsibility of rearing children, no longer consumed by climbing the corporate ladder to success, we have freedom to continue to realize our purpose in life, to develop our talents and use them for the greater good.

Our lifetime of experience also gives us a clearer perspective of what's important in life. We gain knowledge at every age, but wisdom is born of age and experience. As Oprah Winfrey observed on the occasion of turning sixty, "the hardest part of aging really is recognizing the time you wasted and the things you worried about that really didn't matter." The best part, she said, "is being able to be free to be and do whatever you want to." When we combine these two aspects of aging, we realize that aging brings us the time and the freedom to pursue what is important and the wisdom to know what that is. That's a powerful combination, and when we apply the talents, skills, and perspective we've gained over a lifetime of experience to that pursuit of what is important to us, we have the power to indulge our passions, fulfill our purpose in life, and change the world—in short, to pursue happiness.

Legacy and Purpose

When we're younger *legacy* isn't a word we often think about. Most of us are too busy working, raising our families, taking care of our homes, and doing all those little things it takes just to make it through the week. But as we get older the concept of legacy creeps into our minds more and more. How many of us have ever sat through a funeral without listening to the eulogy and thinking to ourselves, *I wonder what they'll say about me when I'm gone?* The desire to leave a positive legacy is a natural human trait, and more importantly, it is a powerful motivator.

In his book *Legacies Aren't Just for Dead People,* author Robb Lucy tells us that we can discover happiness and a meaningful life by creating and enjoying our legacies now. He defines legacy as "something I create that connects and enhances lives now and will continue to positively affect others when I'm gone."

As CEO of AARP, I am the steward of the legacy left by our founder, Dr. Ethel Percy Andrus, a retired high school teacher and the first female high school principal in California. After retiring as the principal of Lincoln High School in Los Angeles, Dr. Andrus began serving as a volunteer with the California Retired Teachers Association. She went to look up a former Spanish teacher whom she had been told needed some help. When she went to the address she had been given and knocked on the door, she was told that the woman she was looking for lived out back—in an old chicken coop. That was all the woman could afford after her food and medicine expenses were deducted from her $40 a month pension.

Dr. Andrus was appalled and decided to do something about it. She was able to help the woman with glasses, dentures, and some additional money to buy food. Then she organized like-minded retired educators and began a campaign to get affordable medical insurance for retired teachers. At that time most insurance companies didn't offer health insurance to older persons. When policyholders turned sixty-five, their health and accident insurance usually was either canceled or the premiums skyrocketed and were no longer affordable. But Dr. Andrus kept up the crusade.

In 1947 Dr. Andrus formed the National Retired Teachers Association, the forerunner to AARP. She began calling on insurance companies, urging them to develop a group health insurance plan for retired teachers. Over seven years she was turned down forty-two times. "They thought I was a crank," she recalled, "especially when I told them I wanted a non-cancelable, budget-priced policy to be paid for by the month with no physical examination. Some wouldn't see me; others showed me the tables to prove they'd go broke if they wrote the policy I wanted. Their data came from people in Veterans hospitals. 'But I've never been in a hospital,' I told them. 'Your problem is that you don't know healthy people.'"

Her perseverance and diligence paid off. In 1955 she finally found a company that would offer a plan to her members, creating the first group health insurance plan for people sixty-five and older in this country, a full decade before Medicare. The plan was open to all members of NRTA without medical examination. The demand was enormous, and by 1957 NRTA's health insurance program was so successful that they became inundated with requests from seniors across the country wanting to know how they could get health insurance for themselves. So in 1958 Dr. Andrus founded AARP to make affordable group health insurance available to all older Americans. But to Dr. Andrus, ensuring that seniors had access to affordable health care was just the first step. To her, AARP was a way to advance her notion of productive aging, to involve older people in society and help them age with independence, dignity, and purpose. This was her calling and would be her true legacy—to help people live a more fulfilling life as they grew older.

Dr. Andrus knew then what we know even better today: that discovering and fulfilling our purpose in life is not only the essence to leaving a positive legacy but also the key to living the good life that we all seek. As she put it, "Second only to the desire to live is the natural yearning to be wanted and needed, and to feel that one's contribution to life is essential."

At AARP we not only build on Dr. Andrus's legacy with the work we do every day; we also honored her with our AARP Andrus Award, which we present biennially to individuals whose work and achievements reflect our vision of a society in which everyone ages with dignity and purpose. We have had many distinguished recipients over the years, ranging from Margaret Mead to General Colin Powell to Norman Lear and Dr. Maya Angelou. This year we honored Mrs. Elizabeth Dole. Mrs. Dole had a distinguished forty-five-year career in public service as a cabinet secretary, a US Senator, and head of the American Red Cross. Then, in 2012, at the age of seventy-six, she created the Elizabeth Dole Foundation: Caring for Military Families to raise awareness and garner support for the people she calls Hidden Heroes. Mrs. Dole is a fearless advocate for the more than 1 million family members who provide care, often day and night, for sons and daughters, husbands and wives who were injured during combat. Often they are the only available, knowledgeable, or trusted person to provide such care. Through her foundation she is drawing attention to this group of exhausted but tireless, undervalued but invaluable caregivers, improving not only their lives but also the lives of those wounded warriors they care for. This work, she says, has given her new purpose and meaning. And she is inspired every day by the people she meets who are caring for their wounded loved ones.

The stories of Dr. Andrus and Mrs. Dole are far from unique. As more and more people move into extended middle age, their search for a more meaningful and purposeful life is being acted out in a multitude of ways all aimed at creating legacy by connecting and enhancing lives now that will continue to have an impact well into the future. They want to use their skills and experience to address social needs and solve problems in their communities, across the country, and throughout the world. Some do this by volunteering with organizations that address social impact in areas such as education, health care, social services, and the environment. And a growing number are engaging in encore careers, seeking jobs that draw upon their skills and experience to address major social needs. An estimated 9 million Americans ages forty-four to seventy are now engaged in encore careers, and another 31 million are interested in doing so.

One of those is seventy-six-year-old Charles Fletcher. I had the pleasure of introducing Charles at the 2014 Purpose Prize Awards in Tempe, Arizona. Marc Freedman, CEO of Encore. org, started the Purpose Prize in 2005 to show the power and impact of people bringing a lifetime of experience to bear in the second half of their lives, and I have the good fortune to serve as one of the Purpose Prize judges. Charles is a former telecommunications industry executive who is the founder and CEO of SpiritHorse International, a nonprofit that offers children living with profound challenges a sanctuary where they can ride horses and work with specially trained therapists to discover their full potential—free of charge. For many that includes walking or speaking for the very first time.

Charles started SpiritHorse in 2001 with three riders and two horses. Today he employs twenty salaried instructors and provides hour-long therapy sessions to roughly four hundred riders every week at his Texas ranch, serving children with disabilities, at-risk youth, battered women, and wounded veterans. He and his staff have trained and licensed ninety-one other centers in the United States, South

America, Africa, and Europe, making SpiritHorse one of the largest and only research-based therapeutic riding centers in the world for people with disabilities. He calls his encore career with SpiritHorse International the most meaningful work of his life.

When I came to AARP in 2010 to lead the work of AARP Foundation, one of the big problems we decided to tackle was senior hunger. We collaborated with four-time NASCAR Cup champion Jeff Gordon and team owner Rick Hendrick to increase awareness about hunger among older Americans and then do something concrete to help them through AARP Foundation's Drive to End Hunger. In 2013 the program expanded beyond the racetrack to include partnerships with the NFL, NBA, and FIFA and now includes twenty-three organizational sponsors and supporters. Through this collaboration we have helped many older Americans find a meal while also raising money for long-term solutions to the hunger issue. By working together, we create a multiplier effect—coming together to reach more people, work more efficiently, and make our collective resources go further. With grants, research, and community outreach, we are helping to make a difference, one community at a time.

It was through our Drive to End Hunger that I met Floyd Hammer and his wife, Kathy Hamilton, from Union, Iowa. Floyd had owned a construction company as well as other successful businesses and simply wanted to enjoy his retirement by sailing the world with Kathy. Then a friend invited them to go to Tanzania to remodel an old leprosy hospital and turn it into an AIDS hospice. With his construction background, Floyd thought this would be a perfect project for them.

So in 2003 Floyd and Kathy made their first trip to Tanzania to the remote village of Nkungi in the Singida Region. They were shocked by the desperation and hunger. Children were dying, and Kathy said to Floyd, "We have to do something. We can't allow these children to die like this."

By 2005 Floyd had purchased truckloads of maize, and the people in the village were told that they could barter for the grain. Although Floyd and Kathy knew the villagers had almost nothing with which to trade, Floyd needed simple things people could easily get, like sand and aggregate for the construction project as well as charcoal for cooking. They were stunned the next morning when hundreds of women came into the village carrying beautiful, hand-woven grass baskets. One by one, they traded baskets for the maize. At the end of three months they had bartered for over twelve thousand baskets and, with that, formed their nonprofit organization, Outreach, Inc.

When Kathy asked the leaders and elders of each village what they needed most, the villagers said they needed four things: safe water, food, medical care, and education. Those four things have become the promises of Outreach. Since that time Outreach has purchased over sixty-four thousand baskets. They use the money from selling the baskets to package meals that are then distributed through meal packaging events with partner organizations like AARP Foundation's Drive to End Hunger. Since its founding in 2004, Outreach has created and helped its partners to create 257 million meals.

What Floyd and Kathy, Charles Fletcher, Elizabeth Dole, Dr. Andrus, and my sister Diane Duggin have in common is that their midlife quests led them on a path of continued growth and development. They used their lifetimes of experience and their skills and talents during their extended middle age to continue to find meaning and purpose in their lives and to create powerful legacies. They are doing things that help people now and that will continue to enhance people's lives well into the future. They have designed their longer lives to make full use of their time and talents and, in doing so, have sparked new solutions that are allowing more people to choose how they want to live and age.

What's Next?

The desire to find meaning and purpose in our lives is not dictated by wealth, income, education level, gender, ethnicity, race, marital status, occupation or profession, or any other demographic characteristic. It's something almost all of us want. But although it is common, it is also very personal. It's something we each experience in our own way. My purpose in life is probably not the same as yours. What I find meaningful may not be what you find meaningful. My pursuit of happiness may not be the same as yours. My definition of the good life may not be what you consider it to be. Yet as we move into middle age, we are all faced with the same universal question: What's next?

"What's next?" is the defining question of our time. Whether it's about work or money, relationships or health, people across the country and up and down the age spectrum are asking the question, "What's next?" For many of us "What's next?" is a tough question to answer. Some of us take this question as an opportunity to re-imagine our lives, to think of all the possibilities we have for financial security,

good health, meaningful work, romance, discovery, travel—
and the list goes on. However, it's also a question that causes
us to face our fears—fear of the unknown, fear of outliving
our money, fear of losing our independence, fear of failing
health, fear of becoming a burden on our families, or just
simply fear of boredom. It can set us on the path to a midlife
crisis or a midlife quest, depending on our perspective and
mindset. Or it can just paralyze us and keep us from moving
forward with our lives.

Scott Strain faced his "What's next?" moment when he
took an early retirement from his employer, a large insurance company in Madison, Wisconsin. His two boys were
grown, married, and starting families of their own. His
wife was still working part time as a nurse, and Scott was
also a long-distance caregiver for his eighty-seven-year-old
mother. Scott said that by following their long-term meticu-
lous planning, the financial part was an easy decision. "That
was really straightforward," he said. "We just sat down and
did the math and determined we could make it work." The
harder part was figuring out what he would do if he retired.
As he explained it, "I've actually thought about doing something different for a long time, but I always felt like I didn't
have any options. Now I almost feel like I have too many options. I just don't know what I want to do."

He wanted to do something meaningful, where he felt like
he was making life better for others. At age fifty-eight, he
went back to college to get his master's degree to become a
college instructor, but he came to realize it was not what he
thought it would be. He enjoyed teaching the students, but
the academic bureaucracy took all the fun out of it. Then a
friend told him about a new website, LifeReimagined.org, a
program developed by AARP and some of the world's leading

experts in life coaching, counseling, and guidance to help people discover new possibilities, prepare for the changes they want to make, and support them as they make it happen. It offered him a map to help him plan the next part of his life.

As Scott began to chart the next part of his life, he realized that he had a strong desire to help people overcome difficulties in their lives. He also loved dogs and had an affinity for working with animals. Scott had developed his love of animals while working for a veterinarian during his summers while in high school, and at one point in his life he had considered becoming a veterinarian. So after talking to his wife and several of his friends, he began exploring ways to marry those two interests. This led him to contact a local veterinarian in Madison for assistance, who referred Scott to one of his clients who bred Labradors for hunting. It was there he found Sazzy, a two-year-old, forty-seven-pound chocolate Labrador with hip dysplasia (thus not eligible for breeding). Sazzy had been in the breeder's kennel for over two years with no purpose or usefulness.

Scott and Sazzy went through several rigorous training programs and evaluations to become a certified volunteer rehabilitation team. This allowed them to visit people in hospitals, nursing homes, retirement homes, and other institutional settings. Scott loves to take Sazzy to visit residents in homes in and around Madison. It brings him great enjoyment to see their faces light up when he and Sazzy walk into a room and to know that he and Sazzy may have provided the only light in their day. "I wouldn't trade that feeling for anything," he says. "Sazzy not only makes their day; she makes mine as well."

Scott has found new meaning and new purpose by designing a part of his life in extended middle age that helps him pursue happiness, and now he's sharing that with others as well.

The Good Life

As more people live longer and better, incorporating an extended middle age into their lives, we are discovering that aging does not equal decline but instead offers new opportunities for growth and development, new chances to pursue happiness, and more time to live the good life. Richard Leider, one of the world's leading experts on purpose (he's sometimes called the "Pope of Purpose"), describes the *good life* as having financial freedom, being mentally and physically healthy, creating deep relationships and a sense of purpose, and feeling like you belong. It also means having the resilience to navigate significant changes in transitions caused by positive or negative life events. Thus, it requires constant revisiting and realigning of priorities in these four areas.

As we go about designing our own lives, we need a new mindset, new skills, and, perhaps most of all, courage. As life expectancy continues to increase, many of the challenges we face can lead us to new points of view and the knowledge and wisdom we need to succeed in the future. Too many people resist the transitions that come with age and never allow themselves to enjoy who they are. I urge you to embrace it and be fearless. Once you do, you will be liberated to bring all of your prior experience and wisdom to design the life you want to live.

CHAPTER 4

Take Control of Your Health

If I'd known I was going to live this long,
I would have taken better care of myself.

—EUBIE BLAKE

When Moira Forbes invited me to participate in a panel discussion at last year's Forbes Women's Summit panel on "The Longevity Paradox: Is Living Longer Really Better?" I thought I knew what I was getting myself into. On the panel with me were Risa Lavizzo-Mourey, president of the prestigious Robert Wood Johnson Foundation, and Laura Carstensen, director of the innovative Stanford Center on Longevity, both women I know and respect greatly. Also there was a young woman I didn't know, Laura Deming, a partner in the Longevity Fund.

Laura turned out to be unlike any twenty-one-year-old I have ever met. At the age of twelve she began volunteering with Cynthia Kenyon, a professor at the University of California, San Francisco, and a pioneer in anti-aging research. At fourteen she enrolled at MIT as an undergraduate physics major to study artificial organogenesis and bone aging. At seventeen Laura was one of two young women to receive the Thiel Foundation Fellowship, which also included a grant of $100,000 to develop ways to commercialize promising anti-aging research projects and extend the human health span. And at nineteen she moved to the Silicon Valley in California and began talking to investors about a venture capital firm to finance research projects aimed at developing new solutions for age-related diseases. That led her to where she is today, a partner in the Longevity Fund, a $26.6 million fund that focuses exclusively on the aging marketplace as well as companies and nonprofits that address key issues affecting seniors, such as coordination of care, chronic disease management, reducing hospitalizations and readmissions, disease prevention and wellness, and public health issues related to aging. Laura's passion, her purpose in life, as she describes it, is to "find a cure for aging."

My first thought when I heard this was, *What do you mean, "cure aging"?* Laura wants to tackle the biological aspects of aging to slow it down in order to expand the human health span. She is a remarkable woman. But even as I applaud her mission, I find her characterization of it as a "cure for aging" troublesome. A common misrepresentation, as we know, is that aging is a disease to be cured, but to characterize it that way discounts the benefits we gain from growing older—the wisdom we gain from experience, the personal fulfillment we gain from forming relationships and pursuing our purpose, and the joy of living and contributing to society. Aging is a lifelong process. It begins the day we are born and continues until the day we die.

The saying used to be that the secret to a long, healthy life was to choose your parents well. But today we know that only about 20 percent of a person's health is due to genetics, and about 20 percent is due to the medical care we receive. The other 60 percent is due to social, behavioral, and environmental factors, many of which we can and do influence by the choices we make throughout our lives—what we eat, how much and what kinds of exercise we do, where we live, the quality of our relationships, whether we smoke, and our ability to handle stress. In fact, making the wrong lifestyle choices in these areas is responsible for 70 percent of strokes and colon cancer cases, 80 percent of heart disease cases, and 90 percent of adult-onset diabetes cases.

The decisions we make throughout our lives about our health and how we care for ourselves have a lasting influence on the quality of life we will have as we get older. Consider, for example, osteoporosis. We know that the condition afflicts mainly older people, and thus, it is commonly thought of as an "aging disease." But we have learned from the researchers at the National Institutes of Health that osteoporosis is a pediatric disease with geriatric consequences. In other words, if you don't get enough calcium when you are young and building most of your bone mass, the damage is done, though you won't see the effects until you get older.

We can make similar connections with cardiovascular disease, adult-onset diabetes, and perhaps other chronic conditions that many people live with when they get older.

Years of being a couch potato, smoking, eating an unhealthy diet, not protecting our eyes from the sun, and other unhealthy behaviors take their toll. And now that people are living longer, we are seeing this happen more and more.

Now that I've properly scared you, let me tell you that this is one of those "good news, bad news" stories. The good news is that the majority of factors that lead to healthy aging are within our power to influence and control. Now more than at any time in history, we have the resources and know-how to take control of our health. The knowledge, research, technology, and constant innovation are all at our fingertips, making it possible for us to shape how we care for ourselves and how we're cared for. Medical innovations and breakthroughs in science are helping us to live longer. The tools and technologies that make it possible to collect and analyze big data are helping us to make better decisions about how best to care for our health, and communities and new technologies are helping us to create more healthy environments in which to live.

The bad news is that our healthcare system is too focused on treating ailments and not focused enough on preventing disease and improving the well-being of the whole person. As a country, we spend nearly $3 trillion a year on health care. On a per capita basis the United States has the most expensive health care in the world. In 2012 we spent $8,745 on health care per person, which was 42 percent higher than Norway, the next highest per capita spender. Yet despite spending more than any other country, our healthcare system underperforms. In a study by the Commonwealth Fund, the United States ranked last among eleven countries (Australia, Canada, France, Germany, the Netherlands, New

Zealand, Norway, Sweden, Switzerland, the United Kingdom, and the United States) in terms of quality, access, and efficiency. Compared to other countries with relatively high incomes, we have poorer health and shorter life expectancy. Americans fifty and over have a higher prevalence of cardiovascular disease and other chronic diseases, and over a third of all children ages five to seventeen are obese, which puts them on track to becoming the first generation to live sicker and die younger than their parents.

We cannot continue with the status quo regarding our health. Good health is the great enabler to a long, happy, and meaningful life. Without it, we lack the energy and drive to pursue happiness, to carry out our daily roles and responsibilities, to work and volunteer, to engage in meaningful relationships, and to stay engaged in society. Health is much more than the absence of illness; it is what gives us a sense of well-being and the vitality that allows us to experience life in a meaningful and satisfying way. To achieve good health, we need to do much more than just meet goal numbers for our blood pressure, cholesterol, heart rate, or blood sugar or fix a loss of function or get rid of an ache or pain; we need to maintain a vibrant lifestyle by accounting for our physical, mental, emotional, economic, social, and spiritual well-being. We have to look beyond the healthcare system to consider the factors that influence our health in our communities, our workplaces, our schools, and in other aspects of our everyday lives.

If we want to experience aging as a time of continued growth and development, we should proactively work to promote physical and mental fitness instead of just treating diminishment. It's not enough to focus on just treating our ailments, though that is important; we also need a much broader focus on prevention and well-being. And that requires changing the culture of health.

Changing the Culture

Dr. Atul Gawande wrote in his book, *Being Mortal,* that "We have medicalized aging, and that experiment is failing us." He's right. Nearly two-thirds of those forty-five to sixty-four suffer from at least one chronic condition, and for those sixty-five and over, it's over 85 percent, with many suffering from multiple chronic conditions. I mentioned the high obesity rate among children, but the highest obesity rates in this country are among those forty to fifty-nine. For too long our leaders have focused on improving the quality of health care, lowering or at least stabilizing the cost of care, and increasing the value of the tremendous amount of money we spend on health care. At the same time, we have gradually begun to address the ways that the social, physical, and policy-based aspects of our lives impact our health and health care. For many of us, good health is a goal we strive for but believe we will likely never reach, and we often see health as separate and distinct from other parts of our lives, not as the foundation of personal fulfillment, happiness, and contentment.

Embracing a more integrated, inclusive view of health as an enabler of our overall well-being would be a huge cultural shift that will take time and the involvement of all different segments of society. It involves not only changing the way we relate to each other within the health and healthcare system but also incorporating how health relates to and is impacted by communities, business and corporate practices, schools, churches, and many other aspects of everyday life. We must also look for solutions there as well as in the healthcare system.

No one has been a stronger advocate for changing the culture of health than Risa Lavizzo-Mourey, president of the Robert Wood Johnson Foundation. Risa and her colleagues at RWJF have devoted a great deal of their time, research, and resources to understanding what it will take to change the trajectory of our nation's health and improve our individual and overall vitality. They have concluded that we need an integrated approach involving collaboration from all sectors of society, not just those in the healthcare system, to address the many social, economic, physical, environmental, and spiritual factors of health and well-being. And it begins with making health a shared value, a building block of personal fulfillment, thriving communities, and a strong, competitive nation. This doesn't mean that we all have the same definition of what it means to be healthy, but it does mean that achieving, maintaining, and reclaiming health is a shared priority, defined in different ways by different entities.

Building on RWJF's work, it's clear to me that to create a new culture that puts well-being at the center of our lives, we have to change mindsets, expectations, and values. This involves four major shifts. The first is from a focus on physical and mental diminishment to physical and mental fitness. The second is from a focus on treatment to that of disease prevention, health promotion, and well-being. The third is a shift from being dependent patients to empowered users of health care. And fourth and finally, we need to get dependable access to care—something many of us don't have now.

From Physical and Mental Diminishment
to Physical and Mental Fitness

When we look at aging as a time of growth and development instead of a long, slow journey into decline and diminishment, we begin to view health as a key driver of our quality of life as we get older. We begin to realize that our health has more to do with the choices we make each day in how we live our lives than it does from an occasional visit to the doctor's office. And as more and more of us live longer and seek to take full advantage of our extended middle age, we are becoming more focused on how to remain physically and mentally fit in order to live life to the fullest. Health is not a separate part of our lives but the glue that holds the different aspects of our complex lives together. It affects how we relate to our family and friends and our ability to engage in work and leisure activities as well as to be active, engaged members of our communities. We don't want to be held back by physical ailments, aches and pains, or mental fatigue; we want to be able to manage the changes in our health as we age, and we don't want to feel too tired to do the things we want to do. As such, we are now seeking more and better ways to take control of our own health.

Under our current model of health care, doctors and clinicians tend to see health through a lens of diminishment— they try to find out what's wrong with you and treat it using the tools at their disposal, such as medications, surgery, and physical therapy. As consumers, however, we're more interested in questions like: How can I avoid getting sick in the first place? How do I maintain my vitality? How do I maintain my health so I can do the things I want to do in life?

Whereas the clinician lens is more about test results, infection rates, morbidity factors, and so forth, for consumers, health is becoming more of a tool for living your best life. Think about hearing loss. To many a doctor, hearing loss is seen as a physical disability, a condition or an illness to be diagnosed and treated. But for us as consumers, it's a quality-of-life issue that affects our ability to live fully each day. It can lead to strained relationships, loss of independence, isolation, perhaps even safety issues. While the doctors are concerned with the medical outcomes, we want to be able to live well every day and continue to be engaged in society. So the question then becomes: How do we translate the medical management and advice into our daily lives so that it can help us live well every day?

As more of us see ourselves as consumers when addressing our own health care, we're taking more responsibility for our own health, seeking more and better information to help us make healthier decisions, and we're increasingly asking our doctors and clinicians to help us understand how to translate medical outcomes into acts of daily living while considering our values, lifestyle, and the impact those outcomes will have on our relationships. We're asking them to tell us what we can do to take more control of our own health, and often that means much more than "take this pill." But more than that, we want our healthcare providers to work with us to help us adopt lifestyle changes that lead us toward physical and mental fitness and enhance our well-being, not just treat our ailments.

Since I started working on this book and thinking personally about a lot of these issues, I've begun to make important health changes in my own life. I'm drinking more water, have cut out all sodas, and am eating more fruits and vegetables. My personal physician, Dr. Linda Coleman, frequently texts me around 5:30 in the morning—she knows I'm up—with a nice little note asking me if I'm walking. I'll admit I don't always stick to her advice, but I recently purchased a Fitbit, and it's a great tool. I exercise more because I can actually see when I'm not active through the day.

From a Primary Focus on Treatment to a Focus on Disease Prevention, Health Promotion, and Well-Being

Most of the time when I talk to people fifty and older, I find them to be incredibly optimistic about their futures. They look forward to having the time and the freedom to do what they want to do and to enjoy life on their own terms. And they have a heightened awareness of the role health plays in their ability to do that. Mostly they talk about having the energy to do things like hiking, keeping up with their grandchildren, taking that vacation they always wanted to take, and just doing day-to-day chores. But they also talk about doing whatever they can to avoid debilitating illness. Most people, as they get older, don't fear death nearly as much as they fear becoming terminally ill or incapacitated, losing their independence, and becoming a burden on family and friends. So they become more serious about finding ways to maintain their health and well-being, avoid disease, and develop habits to promote good health.

That, in part, explains why people fifty and over are at the forefront of a $500 billion consumer healthcare market that is driven by prevention and wellness products and services, which includes vitamins, nutritional supplements, weight management products and programs, fortified foods and beverages, exercise programs and equipment, fitness club memberships, and so forth. Retailers such as Walgreens, Target, and CVS now offer in-store clinics, preventive screenings, and nutrition assessments. And the digital world is exploding with health information and health apps designed to help people live well. According to one study, in 2014 96 percent of Americans with Internet access used it to look up health information. WebMD alone received 150 million unique visitors in 2014, and the two leading mobile platforms, iOS and Android, surpassed one hundred thousand apps, with most addressing fitness or chronic illness.

Employers, many seeking ways to control their rising healthcare costs, are also playing an increasing role in promoting wellness and well-being. Ninety percent of US companies with two hundred or more employees now have wellness programs. These often include gym and exercise discounts, smoking-cessation programs, lifestyle coaching, nutrition classes, free flu shots, and preventive screenings.

The government is also getting on the bandwagon to promote health and well-being. The Affordable Care Act encourages employer wellness programs by offering companies financial incentives and provides Medicare beneficiaries with a free annual "wellness visit" as well as vaccinations and free screenings for diabetes, cholesterol, and cancer.

The Department of Health and Human Services reported that 71 million people in private health plans and another 34 million Medicare beneficiaries had taken advantage of at least one free preventive service such as a mammogram, flu shot, or wellness visit.

What all of this also tells us is that people are looking for ways to prevent disease and promote health and well-being outside the doctor's office. As consumers, we are looking for more and better products, services, and programs to help us prevent disease, promote health, and achieve well-being. Employers, insurers, and government are investing and coming up with new employee wellness programs like those mentioned above as well as other incentives to get us to focus more on wellness and well-being. So why has our healthcare system been so slow to make the transition from primarily focusing on treatment to that of prevention, health promotion, and well-being?

There are some healthcare providers who have embraced what is becoming known as *lifestyle medicine*. For example, Dr. Dean Ornish, founder and president of the Preventive Medicine Research Institute and a clinical professor of medicine at the University of California, San Francisco, has found that a regimen of a whole-foods, plant-based diet; moderate exercise; stress management techniques, including meditation and yoga; and social support can reverse the progression of severe coronary heart disease and may begin to reverse type 2 diabetes and slow, stop, or even reverse the progression of early-stage prostate cancer. Ornish's lifestyle program for heart disease is now reimbursable by Medicare and many private insurers. Lifestyle medicine, Ornish says, "is not just about how long we live but also about how well we live. It reframes the reason for making these changes from fear of dying to the joy of living."

Unfortunately Dr. Ornish is still the exception instead of the rule. Why is there still such a disconnect between the way physicians and clinicians view outcomes and the way consumers view outcomes? The most obvious answer is that our medical system is set up to benefit more when we are ill than when we are healthy. There is no real financial incentive for those in the medical system to embrace preventive medicine. But another part of the answer lies in the nature of the doctor-patient relationship. Doctors, nurses, and clinicians can provide us with valuable information on how to improve our medical outcomes, but we must be able to take that information and put into practice the behaviors that will help us live better every day. We must shift from being dependent patients to empowered consumers.

From Dependent Patients to Empowered Consumers

What's the difference between a patient and a consumer? Is there any difference? Do physicians treat "patients" any differently from how they treat "consumers" of health care? And do consumers of health care act any different from patients?

Many people would say no, that a consumer is no different from a patient, and doctors don't treat them any differently. But I think there is a difference. In fact, I believe it is a major difference that redefines the framework of our health-care system. It's more than just a change in the name; it's a dynamic change in the relationship among all the players involved in providing, seeking, receiving, and paying for health care in this country. And it's time we recognize it.

So what is the difference between a "consumer" and a "patient"? The word *consumer* is an active term. It implies that a person is doing something—using or buying—for his or her own purposes. To be patient is to calmly tolerate pain, trouble, or difficulty without complaining. You probably don't see too many of those people around HMOs, doctors' offices, or hospitals these days.

The word *patient* is a more passive term than consumer. Patients receive. Consumers buy or use. Patients take whatever comes; they endure, suffer, or tolerate. Consumers look out for their own self-interests. They use, buy, and seek satisfaction. So a consumer of health care is one who uses or buys healthcare products and services to satisfy his or her own needs, whereas a patient takes a less active role and just receives health care. So although a healthcare professional may not treat a "consumer" any differently from a "patient," you can rest assured that a "consumer" treats a healthcare professional differently from how a "patient" does. And that's why consumerism is altering relationships throughout the healthcare system.

Consumers don't want simply to *receive* health care. They want to be equal players. They want a partnership with their providers and physicians. Consumers don't want to take whatever comes. They want to have a voice in their treatment. They want satisfaction. They want to achieve the outcome. Consumers don't want to endure or tolerate. They demand quality. And they are looking for value for their healthcare dollars.

So whereas patients often feel that they are at the mercy of the healthcare system, consumers see themselves as full partners in decisions that impact their health and well-being and are empowered to act in their own self-interests. What empowers them? Three things: information, technology, and a strong sense of individual responsibility.

There is no question that information about health and well-being—and the technology that makes it readily available—are driving the trend toward consumerism in health care. Add to this mix an insatiable appetite for this information—especially from aging baby boomers—and we have the ingredients for a significant change in the culture of health care.

From Unreliable Access to Care to Dependable Access to Care

Quality health care is about keeping people healthy and vital, not just treating them when they're sick. In the medical model of health we think of access to care primarily in terms of health insurance coverage. But when we think of health in terms of well-being, we have to think of it more broadly. It's not only a matter of having health insurance coverage; it's also about receiving the right kind of care that addresses our desire to maintain a vital lifestyle, getting the comprehensive and continuous care we may need to manage our health, and having access to the right tools and information to make healthier choices as well as access to nutritious food, adequate housing, job opportunities, and a healthy, safe environment.

Make no mistake about it: having health insurance is critically important. Without health insurance, adults have less access to effective clinical services, including preventive care, and if sick or injured, they are more likely to suffer poorer health outcomes, greater limitations in quality of life, and premature death.

People without health insurance generally are not as healthy as those with insurance. They tend to put off or totally forego needed care and often do not take prescriptions as prescribed—if they get them filled at all. They are at higher risk for preventable hospitalizations and for missed diagnoses of serious health conditions. And if a chronic condition is diagnosed, they are less likely to receive follow-up care, leading to a further decline in their health. They are also far less likely to receive preventive care and to get recommended routine screenings. This can delay the detection of certain types of cancers and other conditions, and as a result, the uninsured have a significantly higher mortality rate than those with insurance.

One result of the Affordable Care Act is that more of the uninsured now have access to coverage. In fact, over 16 million formerly uninsured Americans now have coverage under the ACA. Additionally, the ACA provides more access to preventive services, even for those on Medicare.

The uninsured aren't the only ones not taking advantage of preventive care. Only one in four adults from fifty to sixty-four years old is up to date with basic recommended cancer screenings and other preventive health care. Cancer, heart disease, diabetes, and other often preventable chronic diseases are responsible for seven out of ten American deaths every year and consume 75 percent of our health spending. According to one study, if people got just five preventive services when they needed them—colorectal and breast cancer screening, flu vaccines, counseling to help them stop smoking, and regular aspirin use—we would save one hundred thousand lives each year. It is appalling that this many lives are being lost due to something as simple as not getting screened for a particular disease. As you've already seen in previous chapters, many issues facing older Americans today are complicated, difficult shifts in culture or policy. But getting screened for illnesses is simple and effective, and there is absolutely no reason more people aren't doing it. It's about awareness and pressure. So educate the people in your life about these issues, and when needed, peer pressure them into getting their screenings!

Dependable care also means having access to the right kind of care. I find it astonishing, for example, that at a time when our older population is exploding, only 11 of 145 medical schools in the country have departments of geriatric medicine. Fewer than four hundred geriatricians enter the market each year. Less than 1 percent of nurses and just 4 percent of social workers specialize in geriatric fields. Altogether there are only about seven thousand geriatricians practicing in this country—that's one for every two thousand Americans over age seventy-five. Meanwhile many hospitals, in efforts to control costs, are cutting geriatrics programs. This doesn't make any sense and is totally out of step with our aging society. It's happening because we as a society simply don't value the contributions geriatricians make. Because of their unique perspective, they are able to help older people stay independent longer and to stay out of hospitals, nursing homes, and emergency rooms. More importantly, because they are trained to care for the whole person and not just treat a specific ailment, they contribute to the overall well-being of their patients. As we look ahead to the huge growth of our older population over the next fifteen to twenty years, we need to get our priorities straight.

Changing the culture of health and making the shifts I've just described will not be easy, and it will not happen overnight. Let's face it: it's a lot easier to go to the doctor and get a prescription for a medication we take once a day to lower our blood pressure than it is to eat the right foods, get the exercise we need, and manage the stress in our lives day in and day out that will not only help keep our blood pressure in check but also provide additional health benefits that add to our quality of life and well-being. Nevertheless, culture change will happen. In fact, it is happening, and it's being led by people like you and me because we want to take full advantage of our extended middle age to live life to the fullest. As we change our own mindsets to focus on physical and mental fitness instead of diminishment and think of health in terms of how it contributes to our overall well-being instead of just treating disease, sickness, or injury, we will become more empowered consumers of health care and not just dependent patients. As such, we will demand dependable access to the care, information, and service we need to lead healthier lives that enhance our overall well-being.

This change is also inevitable because we are at a unique time in our history, when the vast aging of our society coincides with unprecedented innovations in biomedical research, genomics, health, and technology. The convergence of these trends with demand driven by an aging population and the development of new health and wellness-related products and services driven by technology and innovation will disrupt aging in ways previously unimaginable,

bringing us incredible opportunities to choose how we live and age in the future.

New Solutions for Controlling Our Health

When William Gibson, the science-fiction writer credited with coining the term *cyberspace,* famously observed, "The future is here. It's just not evenly distributed yet," he could have been describing the revolution taking place in health innovation. Research, technology, and new business models are progressing at an unbelievable rate, resulting in a wide range of new products and services being introduced into the marketplace designed to help us take more control over our health. Among Fortune 50 companies, thirty-eight have now moved into health care in a significant way. For example, General Electric and Intel have teamed up to create in-home health monitors. Google launched a new health company, Calico, to better understand aging and age-related diseases. Verizon has come out with a fall-alert monitor. AT&T has made significant investments in telehealth and remote-monitoring devices. And Nestlé has invested in gastrointestinal health and plans to get into brain health in the future. Dr. Joseph Coughlin, founder and director of the MIT Age Lab, has identified five primary technologies that are driving innovations in products and services: information technology, robotics, genetics, usership, and service enablers.

Information technology is bringing us the Internet of Things, where everyone and everything is connected. This includes products such as Panasonic or Toto smart toilets;

LG refrigerators that monitor food purchases and storage; wearable activity trackers like Fitbit, Jawbone, and the Nike+ Fuelband, which record steps, calories, and sleep patterns; as well as other smartphone-enabled devices that monitor activity and behavior. The Ford Motor Company has even introduced an allergy alert system that provides drivers with an outside air quality analysis, the first of many planned systems that could provide information about air quality, as well as blood sugar level or heart rate monitoring while in your car.

As I mentioned, I've become a fan of my Fitbit. It's helping me to become more active. A recent study of activity and sleep trackers showed that almost three out of four people fifty and over increased awareness of their activity, sleep, and eating habits as a result of wearing these kinds of devices, with nearly half making changes in their behavior. The study also showed that people fifty and older enjoy interacting with this technology when it provides them with constructive and usable feedback on reaching their fitness goals. A key to expanding their use is to make them easier to use and maintain, less obtrusive, and more effective by adding additional features like timely alerts and immediate access to information.

Many robotic devices and applications are already available to help promote health and well-being. These include mobility bots (such as Honda's robotic unicycle and robotic walkers), robotic wheelchairs, social companion robots, home robots (e.g., robotic vacuums and lawn mowers), autonomous vehicle systems in new cars such as collision warning systems, and service robots to dispense medications. Google has prototyped a driverless car. We took our

board of directors out to Google and couple of years ago, and one of our members who contracted polio as a child tried out the driverless car. He said it would change his life, giving him a freedom in getting around he hasn't known in years.

Ever since researchers at the Human Genome Project completed the sequencing and mapping of the human genome in 2003, scientists have been exploring the possibilities and opportunities that genetics offers for improving our health and well-being. Twelve years later we have made significant progress but have still barely touched the surface. Commercially genetic testing services are now widely available. Although they are fun for figuring out your heritage, they are also incredibly useful in terms of family history of genetic illnesses. And as they grow in use, they have the potential to inform healthy behaviors as well as to lead to more personalized medicine for treating disease, determining which drugs to take, and helping to prevent disease and illness.

Usership refers to the growing number of service providers, many of them local, who make it easier for us to perform daily activities. This is known as the sharing economy, or the on-demand economy, and through it we can have the benefits of enjoying daily activities without having to own a car or a bike, for example, or employ an assistant. This includes transportation services such as Uber and Lyft; home maintenance services such as TaskRabbit, with which you can hire someone to run an errand for you or fix an appliance; hotel alternatives like Airbnb; and even pet care services such as Rover and DogVacay.

Service enablers are the growing number of business apps, services, and informal networks that influence the health behaviors of older Americans. These include home health and caregiving services, downsizing consultation companies, and informal online networks.

All of these exciting innovative solutions are changing the culture of health care and giving us incredible new opportunities to take control of our health. But we have a lot more work to do to transform our current "sick care system" into a true healthcare system. We have to continue to push delivery and payment systems away from volume of care to the value of care; lower costs by improving health outcomes, not just shifting costs to the shoulders of patients and consumers; make access to care even more convenient, with retail clinics as a part of this but also including telehealth and other innovations; provide more integrated care, not just by doctors but also by leveraging the potential of nurses, social workers, and mental health workers; and empower individuals to manage their own health with the information and tools they need.

At AARP, we're addressing these issues in a number of ways. In October 2014 we joined with UnitedHealthcare to launch "The Longevity Network" to promote innovations in health care and improve the quality of people's lives as they age. We're focused on areas such as medication management, aging with vitality, vital-sign monitoring, care navigation, emergency detection and response, physical fitness, diet and nutrition, social engagement, and behavioral and emotional health.

Additionally, twice a year we hold "Health Innovation @ 50+ Live Pitch" events that bring together entrepreneurs and start-up companies in the fifty-and-over health technology and innovation sector with venture capitalists, other prospective investors, and consumers who provide real-time market feedback. Since we started Live Pitch events four years ago, fifteen of the thirty finalists have raised $50 million in investments. Two companies dropped out when they got acquired by other companies.

Building on the Live Pitch events, we brought together some of the top names in health care—UnitedHealthcare, Pfizer, Robert Wood Johnson, and Medstar Health—to launch Project Catalyst to put consumers fifty and older at the center of innovation.

And at the end of last year we teamed with JPMorgan Private Equity Group to launch the AARP Innovation Fund, a first-of-its-kind $40 million investment fund that will provide capital to companies focused on providing innovative solutions for health care and aging in place that can improve the lives of people fifty-plus and their families. The AARP Innovation Fund will directly invest in companies that are developing innovative products and services in three healthcare-related areas: aging at home, convenience and access to health care, and preventative health.

I want to address two issues that are particularly critical, because if we fail to come to grips with them, they could undermine our efforts to take control of our health and pose a significant threat to our well-being.

Caregiving

At some point in our lives most, if not all, of us face caregiving responsibilities or need caregiving from a family member and/or friend. Former first lady Rosalynn Carter said it best: "There are only four kinds of people in the world: those who have been caregivers; those who currently are caregivers; those who will be caregivers; and those who will need caregivers."

As our population ages, more and more of us are living with chronic conditions such as arthritis, hypertension, diabetes, coronary artery disease, asthma, and others. Medical interventions, personal adjustments to lifestyle, better health information, and public health advances have made the entire population, on average, much healthier than it was even just a half century ago. Today we can often live quite well with conditions that would have killed us fifty years ago.

Nevertheless, as we reach our seventies, eighties, and nineties, the body becomes increasingly frail, and these ailments begin to take their toll. Many of us need help. The 2012 Genworth Cost of Care Survey estimates that seven out of ten people age sixty-five and over will need some kind of long-term care lasting ninety days or longer.

The first place we turn is usually our family. Family caregiving is the backbone of long-term care in this country—in fact, in most countries. We estimate that the economic value provided by the 42 million family caregivers in this country at about $470 billion a year. And this doesn't count the estimated $33 billion in loss of productivity to American businesses—mostly in lost time.

With our increased longevity, it's become a fact that many of us will spend more time caring for an aging parent or relative than we did raising our children. Many people—especially those between the ages of forty-five and fifty-five—are likely to have the multiple responsibilities of rearing their own children, caring for their parents, and, in some cases, grandparents. We know, for example, that among our 38 million AARP members, 40 percent are providing support for both their kids and their parents. That puts many of us in the position of being both caregivers and, at some point, needing care ourselves.

Today more and more boomers are coming face-to-face with the state and delivery of long-term care as they take on the responsibility of caring for elderly parents or relatives. And by and large they don't like what they see. They are confronted by a system that is complicated, confusing, and expensive.

When we add to this the fact that the number of seventy-five and older households headed by single women is projected to grow from fewer than 6 million in 2010 to over 13 million by 2050, we see a long-term-care system in drastic need of change.

The federal government has struggled for years trying to find ways to assist family caregivers. The CLASS Act, part of the Affordable Care Act that dealt with long-term care, was dead in the water before it ever got started, leaving Medicaid as the only semblance of long-term-care support provided by the government. Now a new bipartisan, bicameral caucus has formed on Capitol Hill called ACT (Assisting Caregivers Today) that is looking for ways to make incremental changes in policy to help family caregivers.

The private-sector market for long-term-care insurance has also floundered somewhat as companies move in and out of the market and consumers are reluctant to purchase policies that generally are expensive and fail to keep up with the rising costs of care. But as innovation takes hold, companies and entrepreneurs see the rising demand and are developing new solutions to address that demand. One example is CareLinx, Inc., founded by Sherwin Sheik.

Four years ago he gave up a career in banking and created CareLinx to help families find a caregiver who best meets their needs and their budget. It's a kind of Match.com for caregivers and families. He wanted it to be affordable for consumers and to pay more to the caregivers to keep turnover rates down, so he designed CareLinx both to save families money and to raise wages for caregivers. Because of his own experience with his sister, mother, and uncle, Sheik saw the caregivers for his family not just as employees but as becoming members of the family, so he recognized the importance of making sure the fit is right.

CareLinx does more than connect caregivers with people needing care; it also helps families and caregivers manage all the administrative tasks of their caregiving needs, provides each client with a dedicated care advisor, and provides families with the capability to monitor the caregiver's activities through tablet and smartphone applications. CareLinx is currently helping more than two thousand families across the country. It operates in the top fifty metropolitan areas with over one hundred thousand professional caregivers.

Another great example of a company that's disrupting this market is Honor. Seth Sternberg, cofounder and chief executive of Honor, became interested in how older people could live better independently when his mother had difficulty driving. Now his mission is to help remake home care. Honor connects a network of professional caregivers with older adults and their families through an in-home screen, an online app, and a new approach that allows consumers to schedule care visits for as little as one hour and to pay by the hour. They recently launched Honor Now in the San Francisco area, an on-demand feature to its caregiver booking portal that allows seniors to request visits on an as-needed basis, enabling rapid responses for patients being discharged from the hospital and in other situations.

Clearly much more needs to be done to address the needs of family caregivers and those needing care. For many of us the transition to becoming a caregiver and the transition to recognizing that we need care is a difficult one to face up to. The recognition that we are losing our independence, that we have difficulty remembering to take medications, or that we can no longer drive is a troubling experience. Likewise, seeing that in our loved ones and realizing that we may need to take action to help is often heartbreaking, and many of us struggle to know what to do. But innovations like those being introduced by Honor, CareLinx, and more are encouraging and open the door for others to find innovative solutions for this growing concern.

Alzheimer's Dementia

Another one of the consequences of a larger older population is that it reveals more disorders and diseases that previous generations hardly knew anything about. Remember, life expectancy in the advanced economies a century ago was just under fifty years. When people routinely live well into their seventies and eighties and beyond, we see some of the debilitating effects age can have on our physical, mental, and even social health.

Alzheimer's disease, for example, was first described over a century ago. Yet it was only in the last generation that we began to see its tragic and costly toll. The patient Dr. Alois Alzheimer described in his article published in 1909 was a woman who was only fifty-seven. Alzheimer's is not caused by age alone, but it becomes more likely with age. According to the Alzheimer's Association, one out of four people aged eighty-five and over have the disease.

As our population ages and people live longer, the sheer number of people projected to suffer from Alzheimer's could mushroom from just over 5 million today to more than 16 million by mid-century and consume one of every three Medicare dollars—unless we find new ways to control the disease. The good news is that progress is being made.

What makes Alzheimer's such a difficult disease is that it takes many years to develop and run its course, and until recently the only sure way to diagnose it was by conducting an autopsy. Moreover, there is still disagreement within the medical community as to what actually causes the disease, making it difficult to design clinical trials to test potential therapies. Much of the research underway is focused on slowing down the progression of Alzheimer's. One study found that if we could delay the onset of serious dementia by five years, we could reduce the number of patients in the United States by 43 percent and save more than $440 billion in caregiving costs. Yet the high-dollar cost of dementia pales in comparison to the emotional costs experienced by all involved.

While research on Alzheimer's and other dementias continues to progress, even though no cures are in sight, we are learning more about how to maintain the health of our brains. Noted brain researcher Dr. Paul Nussbaum (who also works with AARP on our brain health initiative) has created a five-part framework for brain health: keeping physically fit (engaging in regular exercise); learning more, including playing games, doing puzzles, learning a new language, traveling, or learning to play a musical instrument; managing stress, such as by employing relaxation techniques or enjoying quiet time; eating right by avoiding processed foods and bad fats; and being social, like getting involved in something you care about, taking up a new hobby, or connecting to a new community.

All of these are activities we can and should do every day as part of our own well-being. They not only help us to stay sharp mentally; they also fit well into living a healthy lifestyle that leads to healthy aging.

When Jeanne Calment died in Arles, France, on August 4, 1997 at the age of 122 years and 164 days, she was on record as the oldest person to have ever lived. She was born before the Eiffel Tower was built and before the telephone was invented. She was forty when World War I broke out, and by the time World War II came along, she had already retired. When asked at 115 her secret to a long life, she said, "I just kept getting older and couldn't help it."

As charming as that response is, for most of us it is not a very good strategy for healthy aging or for getting the most out of our extended middle age. We have to take a much more active approach. In large part we determine how we age by the choices we make every day throughout our lives, and we have more power than ever before to make choices that will enhance our well-being.

Thanks to a ten-year study by the MacArthur Foundation, we know the formula for healthy aging: disease avoidance, exercise of mind and body, and engagement in life. That means physically—exercise, eat a healthy diet, don't smoke or abuse alcohol and drugs, practice good hygiene, take medications and follow through with health screenings and preventive measures as prescribed—and emotionally, including exercise your brain, stay engaged in life, stay connected to family and friends and develop meaningful relationships.

The challenge for us all is to take advantage of the information, research, and knowledge we have about living and aging well along with the plethora of innovative products and services that are flooding the market to enhance our well-being, and then use them to live well each and every day. Going to the doctor or other health clinician is important and necessary and contributes to our health and well-being, but the simple fact is that we don't live in the doctor's office or in clinical settings. We live in supermarkets, convenience stores, offices, factories, restaurants, classrooms, and playgrounds. We also live in a media society—in front of TV sets, video games, movies, and computer screens. We live on smartphones and tablets. And most of all we live in our homes and, especially, on our couches. The doctor's office is not where our normative behaviors are set, where our habits are formed, or where our peer and other influences take place. Doctors' visits and lab reports can contribute to our health and well-being, but if we really want to take control of our health, we'll do it with the choices we make each day to live a healthier, more fulfilling life.

CHAPTER 5

Choose Where You Live

Life's a voyage that's homeward bound.
—HERMAN MELVILLE

I first met Marion Dudley in 2012 when I went to Charlottesville, Virginia, for the opening of Sunrise Park, a mixed-income neighborhood with a complex of rental apartments, affordable condos, and duplexes with social and community services that give stability to economically vulnerable residents. It was the brainchild of Dan Rosensweig, executive director of Habitat for Humanity's Charlottesville affiliate, and it was built on the site of the Sunrise Trailer Court, where Marion had lived in her own trailer for thirty years. Eight years earlier she was told that Habitat had purchased the trailer court, that they were going to get rid of the trailers, and that she and her neighbors would have to move. She was understandably upset. Dudley, demonstrating a spirit that belied her small stature and a somewhat introverted personality—she usually did whatever she could to avoid confrontation—stood up at the meeting and raised hell. "I think I scared the living bloomers off that poor architect," she said with just a hint of amusement. Her trailer was her home and her neighbors were like family. So she took on the role as the unofficial mayor of Sunrise, representing the residents throughout the long redevelopment project with Habitat.

Habitat for Humanity typically builds houses for families that otherwise can't afford to own a home, so redeveloping a trailer park was a new concept for them. But Rosensweig believed that they could create a new, permanent neighborhood of affordable housing and prevent a developer from coming in and forcing people out. Most of the trailer court residents were older and incapable or unwilling to take on a mortgage late in life, so Habitat offered them the option of either applying to purchase one of the homes or renting an apartment in the new complex. If a resident decided not to stay at the new Sunrise, Habitat helped them find a new home and paid part of the associated fees. According to Rosensweig, this was the first trailer park redevelopment project in the country that did not displace a single resident.

Marion worked with Habitat every step of the way to make sure the development was meeting the residents' needs. "We're like a family here," said Dudley, "and I wanted to make sure we kept that close-knit, family-like feeling of the neighborhood." Of the original sixteen families in the trailer park, two residents passed away, five chose to move elsewhere, and nine took up residence in the new Sunrise Park. AARP Foundation and the Kluge Foundation partnered with Habitat to fund a new community center on the apartment building's basement floor. Again Dudley was instrumental in making sure the community center met the residents' needs. "We didn't want it to be a senior center, we also wanted the young people" she said. "We wanted it to be an intergenerational community center where people of all ages could mingle and take part in the activities." It's become a place where residents gather to socialize and learn from one another. The center offers cooking and gardening classes, acupuncture, yoga, and other activities.

Although Marion admits the transition was difficult at times, and she sometimes misses her trailer, she believes she made the right choice to stay. She looks out over her new neighborhood from her porch, less than five hundred feet from where her trailer once stood, with great satisfaction. She notes with pride that "as residents of Sunrise Park, we now have better housing, it's affordable, we have more services available to us right in the neighborhood, and most importantly we kept the neighborhood together."

What Marion Dudley and her neighbors in Sunrise Park wanted is what most of us want as we get older: we want to reside in a livable community, defined as one that has affordable and appropriate housing, supportive community features and services, and adequate transportation options for getting around, which together contribute to the independence and engagement of the residents in civic and social life. A livable community is a place where people of all ages can live comfortably in good health, get to where they want to go safely, and remain active and engaged in society.

In 2014 the Milken Institute released its second report on the Best Cities for Successful Aging. This comprehensive report focuses on six broad criteria to measure, compare, and rank 352 US metropolitan areas based on how well they enable people to fulfill their potential in their own lives and contribute to society and to others across the age spectrum as they get older. The criteria are safe, affordable, and convenient environments; health and happiness; financial security, including opportunities for work and starting your own business; living options for mature residents; mobility and access to convenient transportation systems; beneficial engagement with families and communities; and physical, intellectual, and cultural enrichment.

Across these broad criteria Milken weighed assessments of eight subcomponents: general indicators, health care, wellness, living arrangements, transportation/convenience, financial well-being, employment/education, and community engagement. Three rankings are included for each city: an overall ranking for the aging population, one for people sixty-five to seventy-none, and one for people eighty and older. According to Milken's research the five most livable cities in America are Madison, Wisconsin; Omaha-Council Bluffs, Nebraska-Iowa; Provo-Orem, Utah; Boston-Cambridge-Newton, Massachusetts–New Hampshire; and Salt Lake City, Utah. Although each of these communities has its own unique characteristics that make it livable, they share common traits such as economic strength, an abundance of quality health services, an active lifestyle, opportunities for intellectual stimulation, and easy access to amenities.

If you want to find out how livable your community is, AARP has developed a Livability Index based on sixty factors spread across seven categories—housing, neighborhood, transportation, environment, health, engagement, and opportunity. Simply go to www.aarp.org/livabilityindex and type in your zip code to see how your community compares with others in terms of the livability factors that are important to you.

Many of us find that as we get older, some things we've always taken for granted get a little bit harder—getting from place to place, buying healthy food, accessing necessary services like health care, going to the beauty parlor or barbershop, and getting back and forth to the grocery store while carrying bags of groceries. Our wants and needs change, but our environment doesn't always adapt to address those changes. These are issues we need to address. We need visible traffic signs, handrails, one-story living, no-step entry into homes and buildings, sidewalks that are in good condition, bus stops with benches, libraries, parks, movie theatres, grocery stores, pharmacies, and places to get together with neighbors and friends that are easily accessible.

Thankfully livable communities are starting to become much more common, and they're not just accommodating to older people—they make life better for everyone. I can't think of anything that would make life better and fuller for a woman of eighty that wouldn't also be good for a woman of thirty or a girl of eight. When millennials are asked what they value in a community, they say it's access to public transit, being able to walk to where they want to go, proximity to shops, green space, good schools, and work-life balance. These are the same things boomers and Gen Xers say they want. The improvements we make in housing design, sidewalk construction, public transportation, and recreation should—and in practice do—make life better for everyone. Well-maintained sidewalks and safe crosswalks help older people with limited mobility as well as parents pushing strollers. Transportation options help residents who may no longer drive get to the grocery store and also help students get to class. Affordable housing helps young professionals live near their jobs and retirees remain in homes they can afford. Intergenerational communities also promote engagement and help people stay connected and avoid isolation. After all, an age-friendly community is not just an old-age-friendly community.

But it's not just affordable housing and transportation that these communities foster; leaders and residents of livable communities make decisions on how to use the land that emphasize their needs and interests. They are proud of their communities and work to keep the environment clean and public spaces safe, green, and appealing. They incorporate principles of universal design in home building and renovation (e.g., wide doorways, zero-step entrances, easy-to-grasp door handles, etc.). And they incorporate what have become known as "complete streets" policies, which require planners to take all users—pedestrians, bicyclists, bus riders, and motorists—into account when designing new roads or fixing existing ones.

Livable communities also spur economic growth by creating jobs and having shopping, health care, recreation, entertainment, and volunteer opportunities closer to home. And communities benefit by becoming more desirable places to live, work, and visit.

Livable communities do more than give people a place to survive; they also create a healthy environment that encourages people to thrive. People who live in socially connected communities—who feel that they belong and are secure— have better psychological, physical, and behavioral health.

Dan Buettner and his team of researchers and scientists have studied the quality of life and culture in places around the world where people live extraordinarily long, healthy lives— Sardinia, Italy; Okinawa, Japan; Loma Linda, California; and the Nicoya Peninsula, Costa Rica. He discovered that people who live in these so-called blue zones share four traits: they eat a healthy, plant-based diet; live an active lifestyle; have a clear sense of purpose; and develop strong social networks. Something for us all to strive for, right?

In 2009 AARP joined with Buettner and the United Health Foundation to bring these principles to a community to create America's healthiest hometown. We launched the AARP/ Blue Zones Vitality Project in Albert Lea, Minnesota, a community of about eighteen thousand residents. Our mission was to weave the Blue Zones principles into virtually every aspect of the community—restaurants, businesses, schools, homes, and everyday lives—in hopes of adding healthy years to an entire town.

We brought in experts to work with town leaders to begin to transform both the physical and cultural aspects of Albert Lea. The town incorporated many infrastructure improvements to make the town more friendly to bicyclists and pedestrians. They created community gardens, new walking trails, and intergenerational "walking school buses" where parents, grandparents, and volunteers can walk children to school as a group. They constructed a sidewalk loop around the town's picturesque lake to entice residents to leave their cars at home.

At the same time, longevity, nutrition, childhood obesity, and diet experts canvassed the town's homes and restaurants, sharing simple tips for healthy eating. Food experts worked with the town's grocery stores to identify and label "longevity foods" such as beans, lentils, soy, oranges, grapefruit, sweet potatoes, pumpkins, apricots, peaches, carrots, and tomatoes. Local restaurant and school menus as well as workplace cafeterias and vending machines were overhauled with an emphasis on longevity foods. In addition, life coaches held free motivational seminars to teach and encourage people how to use their talents and passions to find and pursue their life's purpose.

Of course, in order for this project to be a success, it was important that the people in the town feel motivated to adopt these healthy habits and this mentality permanently so they could continue once we left. Residents loved it and participated in initiatives from walking groups to healthy cooking classes to community gardening. As fifty-two-year-old Moraa Knoll, a Kenyan by birth, put it, "People are connecting more because of the Vitality Project. It's made me feel better about Albert Lea and America." By the time the Vitality Project ended in October 2009, a total of 3,464 of the town's 18,000 residents had participated. The life expectancy of the 786 residents who measured their longevity before and after rose by 2.9 years and all said they feel healthier, both physically and emotionally. Two-thirds of locally owned restaurants added life-extending foods to their menus, and thirty-five businesses pledged to make their workplaces healthier. Employers reported sharp drops in absenteeism and reduced healthcare costs.

The Vitality Project is only one example of how communities across the country are changing to become more livable for residents of all ages. More and more communities are starting to get it. Around the country we are seeing creative local partnerships leading to livability solutions tailored specifically to the unique characteristics of that community.

Des Moines, Iowa, launched its Age-Friendly Initiative in 2013, aimed at building infrastructure to accommodate the aging population, improve walk-ability and transportation options, provide jobs for people fifty and over, promote new business start-ups through an Encore Entrepreneur program, and provide resources for connecting volunteers with opportunities in the community. They also encourage better customer service through an age-friendly certification program for businesses and promote "senior college" opportunities and other programs to strengthen senior alliances with colleges and universities.

The initiative also recognizes the important role that health and community support services play and encourages locating residential facilities near the services that people need; improving coordination of care and services for those over fifty; identifying and promoting greater in-home care options; creating programs that reduce rates of obesity, diabetes, and other chronic illness; increasing mobility and physical activity options for residents; and integrating the needs of people fifty and over into city/county emergency planning.

In Richmond, Virginia, Virginia Commonwealth University (VCU) and Dominion Place, a privately owned apartment building housing older adults and adults with disabilities located near the VCU campus, joined forces to create the Richmond Health and Wellness Program, a clinic located in Dominion Place. The clinic offers care coordination, blood pressure and glucose monitoring, and wellness education to augment the residents' existing healthcare services and to help maintain their health between doctor's visits. The clinic is staffed by students and faculty supervisors from the VCU Schools of Nursing, Medicine, Pharmacy, and Social Work during the week, and they work with residents to develop individual health plans, manage chronic conditions, assist with medications, and comply with orders from residents' primary care doctors. Before the clinic opened, most residents would use ambulances and hospital emergency rooms for routine care and would often take expired medications and use other residents' prescriptions. The clinic helps them avoid unnecessary high-cost services, improves their overall health and wellness, and, at the same time, provides students with practical community-based experience.

These examples illustrate that there is no shortage of ideas and approaches to making communities more livable. What all of these communities and initiatives have in common is that they bring together public officials, private business and community leaders, and concerned individuals to create solutions designed specifically for that community. There is no one-size-fits all solution for making communities more livable; each one is unique, with its own set of strengths, problems, and solutions.

Choosing Your Home

On the surface choosing where to live as we get older seems like a simple decision. In fact, most of us have already made it: 90 percent of us want to age in our own homes and in the communities we know, not with relatives, in nursing homes, or in assisted-living facilities. This makes perfect sense. Our homes are part of our identity. They hold our possessions and our memories. They give us a sense of place and belonging and are our touchstones of personal independence and engagement in community. They are places where we spend time with our family, friends, and neighbors. They make us feel safe, secure, and comfortable. Yet as we age many of us look around at our homes and communities and find that they are no longer a good fit. We may need to adapt or create home and community environments that support healthy aging and continued productivity as well as nurture our desire to lead purposeful, meaningful lives as we get older.

Far too often, however, just the opposite happens. Our homes and communities become roadblocks. There can be physical roadblocks like stairs that we have more difficulty navigating, infrastructure roadblocks like poor street lighting, or roadblocks that stem from personal changes like no longer wanting or being able to drive while living in a suburb or rural area. The truth is, just about anything can become a roadblock to living a full and independent life if we let it. So in creating more livable homes and communities, we must identify and remove the roadblocks that exist in our homes and communities. Or better yet, stop creating them in the first place.

In the last generation or two, homes in America have changed significantly, and mostly for the better. The wooden I-beams that we now use are lighter, stronger, and cheaper than two-by-twelve joists, providing better protection from storms and earthquakes and making homes more affordable for those who, decades ago, may not have been able to afford them. We now have double-glazed tilt windows and amenities like master bedroom suites, built-in vacuum systems, home theaters, and entertainment rooms. Houses, townhomes, and apartments these days are quite different from and generally much more desirable than those built in the 1950s and '60s—with one exception: they don't accommodate their owners as they age. With very few notable exceptions, American housing today has way too much in common with houses built a hundred years ago, when average life expectancy was less than fifty.

Think about it: when life expectancy was only about fifty, most people could manage stairs well enough. Fewer people lived long enough to need wheelchairs or walkers, so narrow thresholds, doorways, and halls weren't a problem. Fewer people grew old enough to suffer from arthritis in their hands and joints, so round doorknobs worked just fine. By and large, people didn't worry about downsizing their homes when their kids moved out because we weren't building McMansions back in those days. Many of those houses are still occupied in neighborhoods around the country, and as new models were built, the designs didn't change much. But today, with more of us living into our eighties and nineties and wanting to stay in our own homes as long as possible, these kinds of homes just don't work anymore.

Most of us understand the need to save for retirement, right? We may not do it or may not save enough (a topic I'll get to soon), but at least we know we should. There's no such awareness about the modifications we might need to make to our homes as we get older. We're familiar with IRAs, 401(k)s, reverse mortgages, and home equity loans, but how many of us plan ahead for home modifications we'll eventually need?

How many of us are installing handheld showerheads, grab bars, and cabinets with pull-out shelves? How many of us do these things—but only after we've been dealing with the frustration for way too long? After all, the value of our home is measured by more than a price tag; it's also measured by its ability to make our home physically comfortable and sustain us through each phase of our life.

For people whose personal mobility is slightly diminished, nonslip treads on stairs and better lighting in the stairwells and hallways can make an enormous difference. So can, for example, installing grab bars in the bathtub and lever handles instead of round doorknobs and removing the threshold at just one entrance to the house. There are many instances where simple and inexpensive additions or modifications like these can make a huge difference.

These kinds of universal design elements accommodate the needs of people of all ages. It's common sense, but we rarely ever stop to think about it. Having a lot of steps leading up to the front door of a house is as inconvenient for a stroller as it is for a walker or wheelchair. Wider hallways, if not needed for wheelchair access, can make a great place to put bookshelves and still leave plenty of room for walking. These kinds of designs make homes more flexible and more likely to be places where we can age in place. With our population aging, it's time to recognize that basic access should be built into our homes just like the wiring and the plumbing.

Getting Around

Living in a community with services nearby and having a home that accommodates our needs are tremendous assets for those of us who want to age in place, but they're only part of the solution. Having a grocery store, a favorite restaurant, pharmacy, doctor, or cleaners only a half-mile away doesn't mean much if you can't get there. Having options to maintain mobility, to get around and do things, is essential.

My mother-in-law lives independently in Washington, DC. She is very fortunate that she is in such good health. Just about every day she walks outside of her apartment building and takes the bus to the metro station, where she boards a train to whatever shopping area or mall she has decided to go to for the day. She does her walking inside the mall, has lunch, and she's back home around three. She's incredibly lucky to have her health and a strong, clear mind.

My father, however, is eighty-seven. He lives in rural Alabama about sixteen miles outside of Mobile. We are trying to convince him to stop driving. But driving is a form of independence for him; it's part of his identity. Some days he drives to Mobile to visit family or friends. Some days he runs errands. I know this independence is what keeps him happy, motivated, and alive. I don't know how he would get around if he didn't drive—there is no public transportation within ten miles of where he lives.

We are a nation that loves our automobiles. Want a quart of milk? Get in the car. Going to school? Get in the car. Going to church? Get in the car. Going to the doctor? Get in the car. Remember GM's slogan of a few years ago: "It's not just your car—it's your freedom"?

That's the way many people still feel about their cars, but the fact is that as we get older, we tend to drive less or, in some cases, not at all. Our increased longevity means that millions of baby boomers face the prospect of outliving by a decade or more their ability to drive. If we don't drive, or if we drive on a more limited basis, how do we get to the doctor, our houses of worship, to the grocery store, to restaurants, to visit family and friends? Sadly, in many cases we don't. In fact, over half of all nondrivers stay at home on any given day because they don't have transportation. And 60 percent of seniors report that there is no public transportation within a ten-minute walk from their home. Many live in areas without sidewalks, especially those who live in suburbs and rural areas. They are more likely to be injured by a vehicle than younger people when they are walking. This is a problem that goes well beyond just not being able to get around; by sitting at home, often alone, we risk becoming isolated and sedentary, which can have devastating effects on our physical and emotional health. I'm not just talking about inconvenience—that's bad enough; I'm talking about the loss of belonging and the feeling of being marginalized, both leading to physical and mental deterioration.

This is the unfortunate result of communities that aren't planned with older people in mind. Inevitably the built-in barriers to mobility—and, thus, livability—cause people to become isolated, contribute to sedentary lifestyles, and, ultimately, force them to make changes they don't want to make.

Even in cities where more public transportation options exist, the buses and trains are organized largely around commuting patterns. Often there are plenty of stops around office parks and commercial areas, and service is frequent during the morning and afternoon rush hours. But if you want to go to the community center around eleven in the morning or you want to meet a friend for lunch, public transportation may leave you stranded or take far too long to be practical.

As I mentioned earlier, happily, communities across the country are adopting safe-streets policies—sometimes referred to as "complete streets"—that focus on safety and comfort for everyone on the streets, including drivers, pedestrians, transit riders, and bicyclists. Research shows that well-designed intersections, sidewalks, bike lanes, and other features can significantly reduce injuries, deaths, and automobile crashes.

Just ask New York City resident Amy Rogers. When Amy moved across town a few years ago she didn't count on having to navigate the now infamous "Bowtie of Death" intersection of Broadway, Amsterdam, and 71st Street on the Upper West Side of Manhattan. Rogers, sixty-six, uses a cane when walking, so getting from one curb to the other before the light changed was a challenge.

New York's Safe Streets for Seniors program solved her problem. The city's department of transportation reconfigured a pedestrian island, extended crossing times, and added countdown traffic signals. Department of Transportation spokesperson Seth Solomonow said, "We're redesigning this intersection from the view of a senior crossing the street. This sweeping safety makeover will bring expanded curbs and islands, upgraded crosswalks and shorter crossing distances for pedestrians." Rogers says she now feels safer and is more willing to use that corner, which she had been avoiding whenever possible. This isn't just necessary in busy cities like New York—think about your own city or town. Are there intersections where pedestrian injuries are frequent? Take a page from New York's playbook and petition your community leaders to make a change.

When we think about creating livable communities that help people thrive and stay engaged as they get older, public transportation and safe streets should not be an afterthought or a last resort for people who no longer drive; they should be the norm so people of all ages and abilities will be able to use them throughout their lives.

Supportive Solutions

Like many communities across the country, Swampscott, Massachusetts, a seaside suburb of Boston, was searching for ways to use its resources more efficiently. The idea they came up with was nothing short of brilliant. They decided to combine the town's senior center with the high school. They realized that the needs of the town's elderly overlapped considerably with those of the teenagers. The senior center, for example, had a popular dance program, and the school had an underutilized dance room. In the winter the senior center had been taking its members on a bus to a local shopping center to walk, but it turned out that the school had a huge field house with a track they could walk on. The high school was one of the community's largest capital investments, so they figured, why not build it to serve everyone, from the children and teenagers of the community to its senior citizens?

By all accounts both the students and the senior adults love to interact. The members of the knitting circle have taught several students how to knit. Kids in need of community service hours help serve lunch at the senior center, and war veterans share their stories about their time in the service with students who are studying the wars in their history classes. Resident Alice Campbell says it gives her a sense of being part of the greater community, unlike a separate senior center, which could at times feel isolated from the community and even carry a certain stigma. "We like to see young people," she says. "It's just a lovely feeling, having them nearby."

Dr. Allan Teel, a family physician in the small town of Damariscotta, Maine (population 2,218), had too many patients telling him, "Don't you ever put me in a nursing home." At the same time, he recognized that there were not many options available for those who needed skilled nursing care. So he conceived of a unique solution. He started Full Circle America, a for-profit telemedicine support program, and it's become hugely successful.

Teel's program uses a digital network of monitors and tools to track their health along with volunteers and paid caregivers to help meet older patients' needs, such as buying groceries, driving them to appointments, and other tasks. By combining these two approaches, he can reduce the number of daily hours that someone needs an on-site caregiver from twenty-four to just two, with an additional twenty-two hours of monitoring done by using a webcam and volunteers.

Patients receive a kit that includes a web camera, blood pressure cuff, and stethoscope to monitor their health. The rest of their healthcare and living needs are coordinated by a combination of paid staff, family, and volunteers. Although the Full Circle America program is not inexpensive and can be daunting for someone on a fixed income, it's only a fraction of the cost of a nursing home or assisted-living facility where the patient didn't want to go in the first place. It may also be a good option for those who aren't in need of full round-the-clock care but also cannot live on their own.

I've been particularly impressed with Rest Assured, a joint venture between ResCare, Inc. and Wabash Center, which uses an array of sensors and communications devices to provide on-demand support from certified caregivers through a touch screen. The system includes the use of electronic sensors, speakers and microphones, telecams in common areas, smoke detectors, temperature detectors, and personal emergency response systems. These devices link each individual's home to remote staff caregivers who provide electronic support. If necessary, an on-call person can be dispatched to provide quick on-site assistance, or emergency services may be contacted. Authorized users can also video chat with Rest Assured clients via Skype or other video-call services.

These are just two examples of how innovative entrepreneurs and organizations are using technology to help people continue living in their own homes as they age. Technology is ushering in an exciting new era of transformative solutions for those who want to age at home, remain active and engaged, and stay connected to their families, friends, and communities.

The Internet of Things, which describes a growing ecosystem of physical objects—web-enabled devices that talk to each other and exchange information through the Internet—is transforming our relationship to our homes and communities. Our appliances, the devices we use every day, our furniture, and even our clothes may one day contain sensors and computer chips that will be able to pass on information to other computers and smartphones. Wearables like the Lively Safety Watch, which looks like an Apple Watch and is just as sleek in its design, can monitor our health and movements and alert us to take our medications. In the not-too-distant future your refrigerator will be able to contact your smartphone, computer, or your car to tell you that you are out of milk. Your home's thermostat will automatically adjust the temperature in your home based upon your behavior patterns—what time you get up, go to bed, or get home from work. Sensors in your carpet will sense that your walk has changed and notify your physician that you are at increased risk for a fall. And you can monitor and operate many functions of your home from your smartphone or tablet, regardless of where you are. Laura Carstensen, director of the Stanford Center on Longevity, says that we are in the early stages of a technology revolution in this space, and in three to five years these innovations will transform the way we age.

While the Internet of Things is transforming our relationship with our homes, the sharing economy is providing a wide array of on-demand services that make it easier and more affordable to age in place. Sharing economy companies like TaskRabbit and Hello Alfred enable us to find people online to do routine household chores like changing light bulbs, taking out the trash, or climbing up a ladder to store something in the attic. Likewise, companies like Uber, Lyft, and Zipcar make getting around easier and more convenient. Uber certainly didn't anticipate how well its services would catch on with people fifty and older, but they have realized the opportunity and are launching a new service, uberASSIST, which provides drivers trained to help older and disabled passengers into vehicles and to accommodate walkers, wheelchairs, and scooters. Lift Hero, a San Francisco Bay–area company started by twenty-eight-year-old Jan Connolly, offers services similar to Uber and Lyft, but instead of using an app, customers without smartphones can call an operator to schedule a ride.

Technology is also a driving force behind the growth of virtual villages. Often referred to as *naturally occurring retirement communities*, these are membership communities that provide a network of services ranging from household repairs to dog walking and yard work or delivery of a prescription from the drug store.

In a way virtual villages combine many of the individual aspects of the sharing economy but also add a volunteer component and a social-networking platform. Members can use the virtual village to schedule meet-ups at a restaurant, concerts, or a potluck dinner at another member's home. The social component of virtual villages not only enhances the member's well-being but also gives them the confidence to continue to live at home. According to the Village to Village Network, which helps to establish and manage virtual villages, there are currently 140 villages in forty states, and another 120 are on the drawing board. As technology continues to drive more and better services to help people remain in their homes, virtual villages will continue to grow across the country.

Technological innovations, spurred by the Internet of Things; the sharing economy, with its on-demand services; and the aging of the population are all disrupting aging in ways we have never experienced before and are bringing us new solutions for aging in place and making our communities more livable. And for many older adults the broader range of mobility options these solutions offer could mark the difference between a future of growth, development and continued engagement and contribution to society and one of decline, diminishment, isolation, and loneliness.

More and Better Choices
If Home Is No Longer an Option

While we focus on innovations to help make communities more livable and offer new solutions to help people age in place in their homes and neighborhoods, we also have to consider what happens when staying in one's home is no longer an option. It used to be that the only options for an older person who could no longer live at home was to move in with family or into a nursing home, but today many more creative choices exist and more are being created all the time.

Cohousing with a Purpose

When Bettye Siegel retired after thirty-four years as an editor at the Centers for Disease Control and Prevention in Atlanta, Georgia, she had planned to stay in her Atlanta home for the rest of her life. But as her chronic bronchitis worsened, she couldn't spend much time outdoors in the polluted city air. Because one of her most cherished activities was gardening, this was a real problem. So she decided to leave Atlanta and move to a smaller town with better air quality. But, she says, the thought of moving to a small town was daunting. "It can be difficult to make friends," she says. "I had grown up in a small town, and small towns can be clannish." Then in 2002 she came across an article in *Parade* magazine about Hope Meadows, an intergenerational cohousing community in Rantoul, Illinois. It was a small town with decent air quality, but it was also less than thirty miles from Urbana-Champaign's thriving cultural scene. It was just what she was looking for.

Hope Meadows was the inspiration of Brenda Krause Eheart, a former professor at the University of Illinois in Champaign. In the early 1990s Eheart was the director of the Development Child Care Program at the university. Her research focused on the foster care system in Illinois, and the more she learned, the more convinced she became that it had to change. When she learned that Chanute Air Force Base was closing near her home in Rantoul, she had a bold idea: Why not take a section of the former air base and turn it into a neighborhood where fifteen foster families could live together and receive supportive services from the other adoptive parents in the community and from on-site staff?

She successfully lobbied the state to award her $1 million to put her plan into action and even negotiated a waiver to have her newly established nonprofit administer flat stipends to adoptive families rather than the more typical payments calculated on a per-child, per-day basis. Then she hit a snag: the Defense Department would only allow her to purchase an eighty-three-block unit of the base, not just the fifteen homes she wanted. *So why not scale up?* she thought. She expanded the program to provide seniors with housing at below-market rates in exchange for volunteering with the Hope Meadows community.

Bettye moved to Hope Meadows twelve years ago at age seventy-one and has never regretted it. Over the years she has volunteered as an after-school instructor, as a groundskeeper for the community center, and, for the last seven years, as a crossing guard. And she has plenty of time to do her gardening.

Both Bettye and Eheart believe that what makes Hope Meadows work is the neighborliness in an arrangement where two vulnerable groups of people come together to care for one another. Older adults find meaning and purpose through caring relationships and continued social engagement, and foster families receive the help they might otherwise receive from an extended family. Eheart says that her program would have folded in two years had it not been for the young retirees. They came from all walks of life and were all there for a purpose: to help the children. She says, "My purpose is to take older adults who want to give back, who want to be really engaged, who want to be good neighbors, and focus them on a group that is highly vulnerable."

Meadows has inspired at least a half dozen other such cohousing systems, partnering older residents with veterans who have traumatic injuries and adults with developmental disabilities. As Brenda Krause Eheart has said, "I am so convinced that we have to do much more to utilize the time and talents of older adults to address these social problems."

A Different Kind of Nursing Home

I can't think of anyone who has done more to disrupt the traditional, institutional model of nursing homes than Dr. Bill Thomas. When Bill attended Harvard Medical School in the mid-1980s the specialty that interested him the least was geriatrics. Surgery had a swashbuckling appeal, medicine carried an intellectual panache, and emergency medicine seemed to combine the best of both worlds. After finishing a residency in family medicine, he took a job as an ER physician in a small hospital in rural New York State and felt like he had found the perfect fit.

Dr. Thomas was just a couple of years into his medical career when a local nursing home director called to ask whether he would consider taking over as the facility's physician and medical director. The answer was an easy and quick, "No." Why leave the ER for something as mundane as a nursing home? The next day he logged a twenty-four-hour shift in the ER, nearly all of it on his feet, came home bone tired, and, perfectly timed, the phone rang again. "Just wondering if you might reconsider?" This time he answered, "Well, maybe . . ." After a quick tour of the facility and with visions of an uninterrupted night's sleep dancing in his head, Dr. Thomas became a nursing home doctor. He quickly fell in love.

He fell in love with the residents, their families, and the staff who cared for them all. These were good people, and they needed help. The facility was clean and well managed, yet something was missing, something big. He began to visit the home in the evenings and on his off days and would sit and watch and listen. His daily journal from that time tells the tale: "The clinical care here is good, very good, but people are suffering and dying from loneliness, helplessness and boredom." He decided to do something about that suffering and, together with his wife, Judith (Jude) Meyers Thomas, created a radical new approach to long-term care founded on the simplest of ideas: *Life is better in a garden.*

Soon the facility came alive with the vibrant energy of children, the songs of birds (actually hundreds of parakeets), lounging, cuddly cats, and the loyal friendship of dogs. The facility had become much less like a hospital and much more like a garden. It was 1992, and this new approach became the original "Eden Alternative." The idea blossomed and spread across the United States and, then, to many countries around the world. In 1999 Bill and Jude, along with their five children aged nine years to four months, took off on a bus tour called Eden Across America. The goal was to radically change every nursing home in America for the better.

It was on that trip that Bill came to understand that many of the nursing homes he visited were themselves rapidly aging and that if something radical wasn't done soon, the old buildings would be replaced by new facilities of similar design, and the entire cycle would repeat itself. Sadly the nursing home model of that era was basically a modified hospital, without any thought given to incorporating the comforts and amenities of home. Pulling out a clean sheet of paper, Dr. Thomas sketched an entirely new vision, one that eliminated the old model entirely. Now known as the Green House model of care, this innovative approach to long-term care is radically changing the care provided to elders, including those with significant needs, all of whom can now live and thrive in a place that looks, feels, and operates very much like a home.

The idea behind the Green House model is to make residents feel like they're living in a regular home instead of a hospital. At the Presbyterian Village of Michigan Green House, for example, each house has an energy-efficient design, ten private rooms with private baths, a community living room with a fireplace, a kitchen, and a dining room. The houses are run by trained caregivers. Doctors, physical therapists, and other specialists come as needed. All of this leads to a better quality of life for the residents and more peace of mind for their families.

Green Houses strike a creative balance between group living (with a trained support staff) and the privacy of ordinary home life. Residents are free to set their own schedules, unlike in a standard nursing home, where most facilities are shared and daily schedules are rigid.

Allowing residents to have autonomy has had obvious positive results: studies show that residents are happier and stay healthier longer than those in traditional nursing homes. And employees, who are now empowered to lead and think creatively, find their work more rewarding—thus lowering the turnover rate.

Today Green Houses are cropping up across the country. There are 173 Green Houses operating in twenty-seven states, with more being developed each year.

Generational Mixing

Most Green Houses cater to older adults, but not everyone wants to live with their similarly aged cohorts. Meg Palley, in her nineties, says she'd hear too many peers "complaining about their complaints" if she lived with them. Instead, she lives in a four-bedroom house in Nevada City with two caregivers who pay reduced rent for services like driving and shopping.

Palley isn't alone. Formal cohousing communities, based on a Danish model developed in the 1960s, dot the United States, and more and more boomers are finding communal-style living appealing. Ecovillage at Ithaca, in upstate New York, is one such cohousing commune, where residents range across the age spectrum, from infants to retirees. And Cheesecake, a cohousing community in Mendocino County, California, founded by eleven people in their fifties and sixties, recently celebrated its twenty-second anniversary.

Generations before us had few options for choosing where to live as they got older. For those who could no longer live comfortably in their own homes, they could either move in with their adult children or other family members, or they could go to a nursing home. But our generation has so many more options, and I can't even imagine the kinds of options my children will have.

New technology and innovations in creating livable communities and age-friendly housing are bringing us new choices and new ways to live engaged, purposeful, and meaningful lives as we age. New smart homes, designed for all generations, allow us to age in place. New living arrangements such as cohousing and virtual villages help ward off isolation. And new types of livable communities welcome people of all ages and foster intergenerational connections. The simple truth is that we're all getting older and we all have to live somewhere, so why not embrace the opportunities that technology and innovation offer us to create places where we can live comfortably in good health, go where we want to go safely, and remain active and engaged in society? The choice is ours.

CHAPTER 6

Finance Your Future

I have enough money to last me the rest of my life,
unless I buy something.
—JACKIE MASON

Let's face it: it's expensive to be alive. And as we are living more active and engaged lives twenty to thirty years longer than our grandparents did, we are going to need a lot more money to finance it. It's no surprise, then, that one of the things we fear most about living longer is that we may outlive our money.

Unfortunately for many of us this fear is a very real one. Here's a shocking fact: over half of all households nearing retirement have absolutely no retirement savings, and Social Security provides most of the retirement income for about half of households age sixty-five and older. And in households where there is some retirement savings, the average total amount is only $109,000. To give you an idea, at the current rate, that amount would provide an income of only $405 a month.

Many of us have not saved enough for our later years. According to a recent survey of workers twenty-five and older, fewer than one in four said they are very confident about the amount of money they are saving for a comfortable retirement. That's a pretty terrifying statistic. Looking across all age groups, only 14 percent have accumulated savings and investments of $250,000 or more. Although many people acknowledge that they have not saved enough for their retirement and readily admit that they need to save a sizeable, though probably unmanageable, chunk of their income in order to live comfortably in retirement, more than one in four say they have no idea how much they should be saving.

The reasons are simple. We're busy people living busy lives. Most of what occupies our minds has more to do with next week than thirty, forty, or fifty years from now. Most of us have never taken the time to sit down and think through what we will need to live on when we are older. Some may find it a daunting prospect. Some feel they just don't have enough time to devote to it right now. Still others simply don't know how to begin to calculate what they'll need because they haven't thought about what they'd like their retirement years to be like: Do I want to build in money for travel? Will I need to take care of my own aging parents? Clearly the time has come to change the conversation—or in most cases, start one!—about preparing financially for our later years.

Changing the Conversation

Why is it so hard to save for retirement? Let's take a look at a typical American family. John and Anne are in their late fifties. They're married with two children and live in Evanston, Illinois. They're both college graduates. John works for a company that sells and sets up computer systems for small businesses. Anne is going back to work now that the kids are in college and works for a temporary employment agency while she figures out what she wants to do next. They have a combined income of just over $70,000 a year and a combined retirement savings of about $80,000.

John and Anne are concerned about the challenges they are going to face as they get older. John has not seen much of a salary increase over the last decade. But he has seen dramatic increases in his cost of living. He has to work many more hours just to make ends meet. And he now expects that he will have to keep working well into his seventies.

With both children in college, Anne and John are worried about how they will earn enough to get them through graduation. They tapped into their home equity when housing values increased to finance college costs. But tuition is now around $21,000 for each child. It increases significantly every year and is becoming harder for them to afford.

They're also spending a lot more on health care. Their premiums increase every year, often by more than any salary increase they receive. The value of their home decreased substantially following the Great Recession and is just now beginning to recover some of its value years later. So they anticipate they will have less money from the eventual sale of their home to supplement their retirement and unfore-seen needs such as long-term care.

Higher costs for housing, education, and health care leave them with less money for food, transportation, leisure activities, and retirement savings. And they now realize they will have to rely primarily on Social Security and Medicare to finance their retirement and health care.

Yet John and Anne consider themselves lucky. Many of their friends lost their jobs in the last recession. It took many of them a year or more to find another one, and most had to accept jobs at lower pay than they had been making. Some have lost their homes. And still others have had to file for bankruptcy.

John and Anne are not alone. The latest Census data show that the typical American family got poorer during the last decade as median incomes declined. Today 15 percent of Americans live in poverty—the highest level since 1993. A study by the RAND Corporation found that increased healthcare spending wiped out income gains that typical American families made over the last ten years. And the *Wall Street Journal* reported that more Americans are reaching their sixties with so much debt that they can't afford to retire.

So how do middle-class families like John and Anne cope? They typically do three things. First, they work longer and delay their retirement, and many who have already retired end up going back to work—if they can find a job. Second, they drastically reduce their standard of living and rely more on government programs to help make ends meet. And finally, they take on more debt—borrowing against their homes and 401(k)s, running up credit card balances, taking out loans, and borrowing from family members. As a result, the average debt of middle-class families has increased 292 percent over the last decade.

Is it any wonder that saving for retirement is not very high on the priority list? Getting by day-to-day and week-to-week is about all they can manage. But there are other reasons why saving for retirement is so hard. For many of us retirement has lost its meaning and relevance. If you're fifty and younger, chances are retirement in the traditional sense has no meaning. Advice from family members and financial planners to save for retirement fall on deaf ears. Likewise the idea of achieving financial security is also a nonstarter. In recent years many people experienced the ups and downs of the job market, the stock market, and the real estate market as well as the impact those fluctuations have had on people near or in retirement. In addition, about half of millennials don't expect Social Security to be around when they reach traditional retirement age, forcing them to bear the full weight of financing their so-called retirement years. So saving for retirement is often viewed as an exercise in futility. What if, instead, we think of saving for the opportunity to do the things we've always wanted to do? What if, instead of saving for retirement, we think of it as saving for life?

Saving for Life

Thinking about saving for retirement as saving for life gives us a way of thinking about financing our future that is more in line with the way we are aging today. Just as in Chapter 4 we talked about a new vision of health that expands from a focus on treating ailments to one of preventing disease and enhancing the well-being of the whole person, we need a new vision of financing our future that expands from saving for retirement to enhancing our financial resilience throughout our lives, especially during our traditional retirement years.

When we approach it in this way we begin to take a holistic tack when it comes to our finances. Our focus is not just on saving for retirement but on tracking where our money goes, building emergency funds, coping with financial pressures, protecting our assets, and becoming more educated about managing our money. These last two are especially important for those of us fifty and older. Only about 30 percent of us consider ourselves financially literate when it comes to understanding capital and financial markets and the intricacies of investment options, and because those of us fifty and older tend to have more assets than younger people, we are more likely to be targets of scams and frauds.

Just as the goal of health is not merely the absence of disease but overall physical and mental fitness and wellbeing, the goal of financial resilience is not just the absence of financial hardship; it's having the financial capability to accomplish your life goals and purpose. In other words, financial resilience means not just surviving your later years but thriving and being able to afford to live the life you want to live.

From Running the Numbers to Visualizing Your Future

When most of us think about planning our retirement or quitting our day jobs, we sit down with our significant other and financial adviser and begin running the numbers. How much will we be able to get from Social Security? From our pension (if we have one)? From our personal savings and investments? And from any other sources we may have? We then figure out how much we think it's going to cost us to live and to meet our basic needs. And then we determine whether we can afford it and what kinds of sacrifices we might have to make in order to be able to afford it. These are all necessary and important questions to ask, and running the numbers can be an eye-opening exercise. But there are only two huge problems with this approach: most of us have never given serious thought as to how much it will cost us to live after we quit our day job, and we are now in a position of playing catch-up because we should have done this kind of planning decades earlier.

When John Diehl, senior vice president of the Hartford Funds, talks to clients about investing in their future, he begins by asking them to consider three simple questions that usually catch them by surprise:

1. Who will change my light bulbs?
2. How will I get an ice cream cone?
3. Who will I have lunch with?

These questions, developed in conjunction with the Age Lab at MIT, sound a bit silly perhaps when you first hear them, but they were designed specifically to help people think about what kind of life they will have as they get older.

So who will change your light bulbs? This gets to the larger question of where you will live. Most of us want to remain in our homes and communities, but in order to do that, we have to consider how we will handle the everyday tasks that come with living in and maintaining our own home. Can you handle them yourself? Can you rely on the help of a neighbor or family member? Will you need to hire someone to help? If so, at what cost?

Now, how will you get an ice cream cone? Assuming you want to continue to enjoy the simple pleasures in life, how will you get around to enjoy them? Will you continue to own and operate a car (and for how long)? Use public transportation (if it's available)? Rely on friends to take you? Take a taxi or use a transportation service? All of these have cost implications.

And finally, who will you have lunch with? This question is about maintaining your social connections as you get older and what it will take to do that. It's not the kind of social network like Facebook, but a real one—friends you see regularly who contribute to a healthy and active lifestyle. It's the people you get together with at the local coffee shop, the people you go to the movies and concerts and shopping with, your friends at church or in your book club.

Many of us have trouble envisioning our future selves and what our lives will be like as we get older. We have dreams and aspirations of how we want to live, but it often seems like we're talking about a different person. We're so wrapped up in our day-to-day living that the idea of preparing now for our future lives is not a high priority. We tell ourselves, *I'll think about that tomorrow.* And before we know it, tomorrow is here and we're woefully unprepared.

In 2013 Bank of America came up with a unique method to visualize the retired life people want to lead and to motivate them to save more now to achieve it. It's an app that digitally

ages users' portraits to motivate them to increase their retirement contributions. Alongside the aged photos are statistics about the cost-of-living increases they could expect
as they reached a certain age and the projected costs of milk,
gas, utilities, and other consumer goods.

The app is based on a series of studies conducted at Stanford University that found that people were more likely to
consider allocating more money to retirement after view-
ing progressively aged photos of themselves. In one of the
studies fifty people were shown an aged or current picture
of themselves and then asked to allocate a hypothetical
$1,000 among four choices: a checking account, a fun and
extravagant occasion, a retirement fund, or buying something nice for someone. Participants who viewed the aged
photo said they would put significantly more money in the
retirement account ($172) than those who viewed a current
photo ($80).

Putnam Investments, the second-largest provider of 401(k)
plans in the United States, has tried using peer pressure to
get people to save more. They have pioneered an online tool
to give customers a snapshot of how their savings measure
up to those of their peers (other Putnam customers of similar
age, gender, and income). Using projections, it models how
their numbers would change if they set aside more money
from their paycheck and allows them to make that change in
a few clicks. Putnam calls it the Joneses Tool, as in "Keeping
up with the Joneses." And it seems to be catching on. In a
sample of ten thousand users, nearly a third used the social
comparison tool and adjusted their salary deferral level, resulting in a 28 percent average increase in the amount set
aside for retirement.

The point is, regardless of how you do it, the key to effectively planning for life is to visualize what you want your life to be like. It goes beyond money alone. It involves an integrated and holistic approach to living the life you choose as you get older. Nevertheless, it is still true that the more money and resources you have, the more choices you will have.

Creating a New Pathway to Financing Your Future

A key problem each of us faces in trying to make our money last throughout our longer lives is that the model that has existed for financing traditional retirement for a generation doesn't work anymore. It simply doesn't fit the way we live and age today. We need to create new models so that as we get older we have the financial resources and opportunities to match our longer life expectancy and desire to live a more vibrant, active lifestyle.

The Three-Legged Stool

When many in our parents' generation retired, they had income from Social Security, a modest but stable pension, and some personal savings they had accumulated over the years. This was the classic model of the three-legged stool of retirement income, represented by Social Security, individual savings, and employer-provided pensions. The three-legged stool metaphor held that if people had these three sources of retirement income, they could balance the financial demands of their retirement years and not outlive their money.

Those fortunate enough to have income from all three sources found that the three-legged stool provided them with adequate income during their retirement years to live a decent lifestyle and do many of the things they wanted to do.

Things have changed over the years, and the three-legged stool no longer works to symbolize retirement income for Americans nearing retirement age today. As we have discussed, many in our generation do not envision sitting out retirement on a three-legged stool, or any other kind for that matter. In fact, the word *retirement* doesn't even resonate with many in our generation. We think of it more as a transition, as just having the freedom to do what we want, where we want, when we want. We expect to be active, engaged, and working either full or part time in some capacity.

Many of us are still drawn to the idea of traditional retirement, but many also see it as a stagnant concept, more passive than active. In the traditional model retirement is seen as a time of drawing down our assets, not building up more. That's why older persons are so often seen as a drain on society. We're seen as taking money out of Social Security, not paying in. We're seen as taking money out of the pension system, not adding to it. In reality, with more of us working beyond traditional retirement age, we're doing both.

Another reason the three-legged stool no longer works is that for all intents and purposes, two of the legs—pensions and savings—have become one. The defined benefit pension plans that once formed one leg of the stool and were a hallmark of the previous generation's retirement income are becoming relics. The way these plans work is that your employer saves a certain amount for your retirement as an employee benefit. The amount is usually based on your time on the job and salary history. The employer invests and manages the money, and when you retire you are entitled to a defined amount each month for the rest of your life. But fewer and fewer employers offer these defined benefit plans anymore. From 1980 to 2008 the percentage of employees enrolled in defined benefit pension plans fell from 38 percent to 20 percent. By 2011 it was down to 14 percent, and the number is continuing to decline.

Instead, many employers have turned to defined contribution plans such as 401(k) plans. This is a retirement account set up by the employer that allows you to invest a certain amount of your salary in the stock market. Some employers will match the amount you put in up to a certain percentage or limit, and they will offer select investment options, but for the most part it's up to you put the money aside and manage it properly. It's called a defined contribution plan because the amount you put in is a defined amount; the amount you collect when you begin withdrawing is not. So a defined contribution plan is simply another way for you to accumulate personal savings.

One other aspect of the change from defined benefit plans to defined contribution plans is that it fundamentally shifts the responsibility and the risk from the employer to the employee. Unlike employers, most of us cannot afford to hire professional fund managers to manage our retirement accounts, so we have to rely on those in the financial services industry and our own knowledge. We not only have to learn about prudent investing; we also have to be on the lookout for scam artists who often prey on individual investors.

So with each of us individually taking on more of the risk for accumulating and managing our retirement accounts, with life expectancy and healthy life expectancy increasing, and with more of us wanting to be active and engaged during our traditional retirement years, including continuing to work in some capacity, we need to create new models and new solutions for financing the kind of future we want and making our money last.

The Four Pillars

The three-legged stool model has become a two-legged stool and no longer provides the support we need to live well during our extended middle age and beyond. Building financial resilience throughout our lives requires a new model based on four strong pillars: (1) Social Security, (2) pensions and savings combined, (3) health insurance, and (4) earnings from work. This new model is much more in line with the way we are living and aging today.

Social Security

Just as Social Security was the cornerstone of the three-legged stool, it is far and away the most important pillar in our new model. Social Security insures families against the loss of income due to retirement, disability, or death. It is the foundation of financial resilience in our later years, and in 2013 it kept one-third of older Americans out of poverty. It is the primary source of income for nearly half of all Americans ages sixty-five and older and provided benefits to about 59 million people in 2014.

The amount you receive in Social Security retirement benefits is based on your earnings history and when you start to collect benefits. The average Social Security benefit is about $15,720 per year ($1,310 a month) at full retirement age, and the maximum benefit is $41,880 per year ($3,490 a month) at full retirement age. Your benefits can increase if you take them after your full retirement age and can decrease if you take them before your full retirement age (as early as age sixty-two).

Social Security is also much more than a retirement benefit; it also provides a survivor's benefit and long-term disability protection. For a thirty-year-old worker earning a median salary who is married with two children, the survivor benefit is equal to a life insurance policy worth $476,000, and the disability protections are valued at $329,000. Social Security has other features that distinguish it from other sources of retirement income such as pensions, 401(k) plans, and personal savings. Benefits are earned, portable, guaranteed, universal, and protected against inflation. In fact, Social Security is the only part of retirement income that is guaranteed.

There is currently enough money in the Social Security trust funds to pay out full benefits until 2034. At that point there will still be enough to pay 79 percent of benefits, and 73 percent of benefits in 2089. Individual support for Social Security is high across all age groups, and addressing its long-term solvency is viewed as a major policy priority. We will address the policy implications of this in Chapter 8.

Pensions and Savings Combined

Increasing private savings—whether through a 401(k), an IRA, or through other means—is critical to achieving financial resilience in later life. Although over two-thirds of today's workers say they expect to receive retirement income from an employer-sponsored savings plan, an IRA, and other personal savings and investments, many retirees and workers nearing traditional retirement age have very little saved. About half of all households aged fifty-five and over do not have any retirement savings (for example, a 401(k) plan or IRA), nor do they have access to a retirement savings plan through their employer. Adding to the problem, many of those who do have a retirement savings plan believe they will receive a much higher income from their plan than they actually will. The message here is clear: save, save, and save some more!

Health Insurance

It is simply a fact: no one can be financially resilient in to-day's world without adequate insurance to help cover the high cost of health care. In fact, planning for and manag-ing healthcare expenses ranks as one of our top financial concerns as we get older. Those of us fifty and older account for the majority of the $3 trillion spent on health care in the United States today, and the amount we spend on health care continues to go up as we get older. Out-of-pocket healthcare costs continue to consume more of the income of people sixty-five and over, even with Medicare (which is expected to increase from $500 to $800 billion over the next decade). And many of us are beginning to realize that because of the high cost of health care, without adequate health insurance we are one health emergency or prolonged illness away from financial ruin. So without adequate health insurance, we can never achieve the financial resilience we need to live the kind of life we seek as we get older. The Affordable Care Act is helping to solve this problem, with millions more people now having access to health insurance, but too many still don't have coverage.

Earnings from Work

Today work is considered a key source of income during our traditional retirement years. Almost half of all employees aged forty-five to seventy envision working well into their seventies and beyond. For some this is a choice; for others a necessity. But work doesn't necessarily mean continuing in the same job for forty hours a week. Some people work part time, some shift to less stressful jobs, others start their own businesses or freelance, and still others take advantage of new opportunities being created in the shared economy by taking on "gig" jobs. I discuss work in detail in the following chapter.

New Solutions and Tools for Financing Our Future

Creating a new pathway to finance our future based on four strong pillars can be a daunting challenge, but fortunately new innovative solutions and tools are emerging to help us in our quest for financial resilience. The fast-growing shared economy is not only helping us to live better; it's also providing new sources of income. Employer-provided financial wellness programs are helping us better prepare to meet the financial needs of a longer, more active life. Mobile technology is providing us with tools that make it easier to access and manage our money. And new tools are available to help protect us against financial fraud.

Leveraging the Shared Economy

Janice Tharaldson, a sixty-three-year-old single woman in Louisville, Kentucky, was having trouble making ends meet. For three years she had been renting out a room to a tenant in her house to supplement her small pension and Social Security benefits. She readily admits it was not a good situation, and she wanted to find another way to earn extra money. Her home was badly in need of repairs, and her kitchen appliances were on their last leg. Then she heard about Airbnb, a home-sharing service that makes it easy to open your home to someone for a profit.

Janice decided to give it a try a year and a half ago in April, thinking she could rent a room to someone coming into Louisville for the Kentucky Derby. "Well, it just took off," she says. "Now I rent one to three rooms, sometimes even my studio. I'm very reasonable—$30 to $35 a night—because I want to be in service to those like me who squeezed through the recession and are still pinching pennies. Both young adults and seniors are affected in this way. The more senior guests usually get a push from their kids or grandkids to try it. They often come to visit their extended families without being underfoot. I also have guests here visiting their parents who are in nursing homes or assisted living places nearby." Once her Airbnb business reached a certain level of stability and income, she felt confident enough to take out a home equity line of credit and do some major repairs to her home, including the roof, gutter repairs, painting, and fence work.

Airbnb began as a service designed for millennials, but Anita Roth, head of policy research, says about one in four hosts in the United States are over fifty. "It's a draw for all ages, but specifically the over-fifty crowd, where people are starting to become empty nesters and transition to fixed income," she says.

A recent company survey found that among hosts fifty and over, about half rely on their Airbnb income to make ends meet, and more than 30 percent say hosting helps them afford to stay in their homes. Additionally, people fifty and over are increasingly using Airbnb to book rooms when they travel, helping them to keep costs down and make their money go farther. Airbnb says that it now has a million hosts over sixty around the world, accounting for 10 percent of all their hosts. Not only do the hosts derive an income, but this also helps them to remain socially active.

Janice is just one example of the growing number of people fifty and over who are leveraging the emerging sharing economy to both boost their income by renting out their assets, including their time and skills, and to make their money go farther by purchasing services on demand and only when they need them.

A study released by the professional services firm PricewaterhouseCoopers found that 19 percent of US adults have engaged in the sharing economy as either a buyer or seller. Among sellers, roughly one in four are over fifty. They estimate the size of the sharing economy to be $15 billion and that it will grow to $355 billion by 2025. Other examples of companies that attract people fifty and over to the sharing economy are:

- **Uber:** The largest of the increasingly popular ride-sharing services. Uber estimates that about half of their drivers are over forty, and one in four are fifty or over.

- **RelayRides:** A service that connects car owners with people looking for cheap rentals. Scott Ullerich, fifty-seven, earns a steady paycheck through his HR job at an aerospace company while renting his 2010 Kia Soul on RelayRides, earning an average of $400 to $450 a month letting his ride. "The sharing economy is my retirement plan," Ullerich says. "If I can figure out enough of these little side businesses, I can probably retire sooner rather than later."

- **TaskRabbit:** TaskRabbit connects people with specific jobs to be done—handiwork, babysitting, moving, house cleaning—with others willing to perform them for a fee. William Daub, sixty-three, turned to Task-Rabbit to supplement his pension and ease withdrawals from his 401(k) after he was laid off last year. He now charges $49 an hour to assemble IKEA furniture.

- **ShareZen:** ShareZen markets a software tool that coordinates guests, co-owners, and renters sharing a plane, house, or boat. "Most of our customers are about retirement age," says ShareZen cofounder Shawn Kemp. "Sharing larger ticket items allows them to continue to enjoy luxuries while paying just a portion of the costs."

- **DogVacay:** A service for finding a reliable person to board your pet while you're on vacation. Over twenty thousand dog hosts have signed up in the United States and Canada, and about one-third are over fifty.

- **HouseCarers, Trusted Housesitters, and so forth:** There are a slew of housesitting websites, both here and in Europe. Many house-sitting retirees use the service to underwrite their world travels.

As a primary source of income, the sharing economy is probably not the most stable or reliable means of supporting a family. Many of the costs of ownership, which would normally be borne by the company, are the responsibility of the individual. Most jobs don't have any benefits included (e.g., health insurance, pensions, or 401(k) plans), nor are they part of the formal employment sector where labor laws protect workers. Nevertheless, the sharing economy can be a way to bring in extra money when expenses threaten to exceed retirement income from IRAs, pensions, Social Security, and so forth. It can also be a lucrative side gig, adding to savings in preparation for retirement.

Financial Wellness Programs

Employers are increasingly recognizing that it's in their best interest to help workers make sense of their financial concerns. Money is not only a major source of stress; almost a quarter of employees say that personal finance issues are an everyday distraction, which can make them less productive at work. Having seen the positive impact that wellness programs focused on health have on their productivity, more employers are now creating financial wellness programs as an additional employee benefit to help their employees achieve financial well-being by minimizing financial stress, building a strong financial foundation, and creating a financial plan that puts them on track to meet their future financial goals.

One of the first organizations to adopt a financial wellness program was the National Football League Players

Association (NFLPA). Dana Hammonds, director of player services and development at the NFLPA, says the financial wellness program has helped players increase their chances of having successful transitions to their second careers after football.

The NFLPA's financial wellness program offers an online learning center, a phone line for money help, and a regular assessment of NFL players' financial well-being. Assessments showed that almost all NFL players wanted to know more about investing and how to handle requests from family and friends asking for money. Rookies were most interested in advice on buying health insurance, and veterans were more interested in guidance on estate planning.

Financial wellness programs are not just about retirement planning; they also help employees protect against more immediate risks, including loss of income due to premature death, illness, injury, or unemployment as well as unanticipated out-of-pocket medical and nonmedical expenses. Any of these could cripple a person's financial future, forcing him or her to dip into a 401(k) or to rely on credit to meet everyday expenses.

Mobile Technology

Almost all major financial institutions now offer access to financial accounts, products, and services through smartphones and mobile technology. USAA, for example, has been a leader in financial technology, adding innovative mobile features and functionality so members can access their accounts how and where they want. They were the first company to enable their members to use biometrics— face or voice recognition technology for identification purposes—when logging into accounts. This not only made it easier and more convenient to access USAA accounts when and where the customer prefers but also added an extra layer of security. We're now seeing services expand as providers create more mobile and budgeting apps that integrate savings, investing, payments, discounts, and other functionality. This allows users to create a more comprehensive financial profile and get real-time feedback about their financial transactions.

It almost goes without saying that many of these financial tools and innovative mobile technologies are focused on people who are wealthy, those with discretionary assets, those who are able to save, and those who can generate fees to providers.

Protections Against Fraud

Americans fifty and over have a high level of concern about fraud and identity theft, and with good reason. Identity theft, investment fraud, and other financial scams cost Americans $18 billion in 2014. People fifty and over are often targets because they tend to have more assets. Varying estimates show that fraud affects about 10 percent of people to varying degrees. Nevertheless, it is a key reason why many people choose not to adopt new mobile banking technology and other solutions.

As such, financial institutions and other financial service providers recognize the importance of preventing fraud and identity theft among their members and customers. They understand that a loss of trust due to a security breach will hurt their relationships with customers and their revenues.

One of the solutions that is now becoming more prevalent in the United States (though it's been working in Europe for years) is credit-card chip technology. You may have noticed that small metallic squares have been showing up on your credit cards. They're fraud-prevention chips that require cards to be dipped, instead of swiped, during a transaction. The strip-replacing chip is intended to make *in-person* purchases safer because they cannot be duplicated as effectively or as easily as a magnetic stripe. That means criminals will have a tougher time making counterfeit cards—which account for about a third of all fraud—by using stolen data. Chip technology, however, will not help with "card not present" fraud, such as online purchases. It also will not help with the kinds of data breaches that have embroiled retailers like Target and Home Depot.

Technology is also being employed in other ways to help combat fraud. For example, True Link Financial, a startup funded through the Aging2.0 GENerator program, provides a Visa debit card that can be used to alert the cardholder (and authorized family members or caregivers) to unusual financial activity.

Founder Kai Stinchcombe hatched the idea about five years ago after he and his family discovered that his grandmother was writing as many as seventy-five checks to fake charities every month. "She went very quickly from $50 a month to $50 a day," he says. "She's a retired schoolteacher living in Indianapolis. She can't afford to give $50 a day; in fact, that was about how much she was living on entirely."

Financial institutions' standard advice to families like his is to seize control of his grandmother's banking through power of attorney or a conservatorship, whereby she would be stripped of her checkbook and financial independence. "It's this binary 'now that she can't manage her money, she can't access her money,'" he says. For Stinchcombe's family, placing his grandmother in a financial straitjacket wasn't an option: "Narrowing her world so sharply because of a specific kind of forgetfulness was just unacceptable to us."

True Link lets people with dementia and Alzheimer's like his grandmother maintain their autonomy with certain safeguards. Limits can be placed on transactions such as cash withdrawal amounts, how many magazine subscriptions are placed, and how many over-the-phone contributions are made—all detected with True Link software. "With the advent of sophisticated software," Stinchcombe says, "you can create something that is personalized and yet scalable."

Stinchcombe sees the service, which costs $10 per month, as a benevolent form of assisted living, preserving both independence and quality of life, even if it does involve a user coming to terms with declining cognitive ability. "People think about independence in the wrong way—that independence is not needing any support, rather than having the support you need."

EverSafe is another company leveraging technology to monitor unscrupulous financial activity. Its defense network detects unauthorized credit card use, unusual cash withdrawals, changes in spending patterns, identity fraud, and the like. As with True Link, seniors can assign trusted advocates to help monitor accounts. The service costs $7.99 to $22.99, depending on the level of scrutiny.

At AARP we established a Fraud Watch Network to track the latest scams and alert you to the most prevalent ones in your area. It shows you how con artists steal your money and provides a phone number you can call to talk to volunteers who are trained in how to spot and report fraud.

There's no doubt that as technology continues to advance, fraud will also continue to evolve, so it will be up to all of us to be diligent in finding new ways to combat it and protect our assets.

Not only are we living longer and better than previous generations, we also face a financial landscape that is much more complex, challenging, and continuing to change at a quick pace. We're living and aging differently. The old models of saving for retirement don't work in today's world. Even the concept of saving for retirement seems passé. We need new models that empower us to save so we will have the financial resources to do the things we want to do in later life and the financial resilience to meet our financial needs along the way, regardless of what kinds of barriers we find ourselves confronted with.

Although we face an increasingly complicated financial world and the challenge of not outliving our money, we are disrupting the financial marketplace with emerging technologies, innovative business models, and new providers redefining the landscape and giving us more alternatives to traditional financial practices. These changes are empowering us to take more control over our financial futures, to make more informed financial decisions, and to create more choices for how we want to live and age. With increased choice comes increased responsibility. We have to become better educated about how our financial systems and structures work. We have to take more responsibility for saving, managing, and accumulating our own financial resources. And we have to change our mindsets to take a more holistic approach to financing our futures.

CHAPTER 7

Put Your Experience to Work

There is no such thing as work-life balance.
There are work-life choices, and you make them,
and they have consequences.

—JACK WELCH

Five years ago I had a decision to make. After nearly twenty-five years of government service, I was offered an opportunity to leave my position of chief operating officer of the Library of Congress and become the president of AARP Foundation. I had always said that after government service I wanted to lead a foundation, but I never really took any action to accomplish this goal. And so the opportunity presented itself. My daughter was in college. My son was grown. My husband had just retired, though he was doing consulting work. If I had followed the conventional wisdom of my parents' generation—and the advice of many of my colleagues and friends—I would have just retired. There was just one thing: I wasn't ready to retire. I just wanted to do something different, something where I could really make a difference.

So I set about exploring my options and ultimately joined AARP first as president of AARP Foundation, then as chief operating officer, and now its CEO.

I shudder to think that I almost missed the opportunity because I had this voice stuck in my head that said the social norm at this stage of my life was to play it safe and retire from public service. Fortunately I didn't listen. And today millions of people like me aren't listening either.

My story is not unique—a number of my former colleagues have followed a similar path. I'm sure we all know people who have adapted their work schedules, started their own business, or gone into a completely different line of work. Some volunteer. Many have joined the nonprofit sector. Others just love what they do and are working in their same jobs past what we think of as the traditional retirement age. All are evidence of the changes in America's workforce.

As those of us fifty and older explore new possibilities and seek new opportunities to grow, learn, and discover, we're focused on living, not just on aging—not just on what we need but also on what we want. We no longer live to work—we work to live. Instead of planning for ten to fifteen years of traditional retirement, we're looking ahead to three, four, or more decades of engaging and rewarding life.

Go into virtually any community in the country today and you'll find people fifty and older preoccupied with the same fundamental challenges: How do I balance my world of life and work? How do I find happiness and peace of mind in a world turned upside down by fast and constant change? How do I plan for life and work for the next ten, twenty, thirty, or even more years?

For many of us the path to happiness and peace of mind is constantly shifting. We are reimagining our path to the future and constantly adjusting it to achieve our evolving goals and dreams. And for most of us that path leads right through the workplace.

The American workforce is aging. US employees sixty-five and older now outnumber teenagers in the workforce for the first time since 1948. In 2002 workers fifty and over made up about 25 percent of the workforce. By 2012 they were nearly a third. And by 2022 they are projected to be almost 36 percent of the total workforce. This trend isn't likely to change anytime soon. In 2014 over one in three workers expects to keep working well into what is considered traditional retirement age, either out of choice or necessity. Although many of us will work because we need the money, we are also driven by our desire to continue to contribute to society and to find meaning in our lives, and work does that for us.

Regardless of the reason, our continued participation in the workforce is good news for employers. As the fifty-and-over segment of the workforce is growing, many employers report having trouble recruiting and retaining qualified workers. The Manpower Group 2014 Talent Shortage Survey found that 40 percent of US employers reported difficulty in filling jobs. Areas where US employers are having trouble filling jobs include skilled trades, restaurant and hotel staff, sales representatives, teachers, drivers, accounting and finance staff, laborers, IT staff, engineers, and nurses.

Fortunately many of today's workers want to work and want viable work options later in life. So in light of the declining proportion of younger workers and the projected shortages of talent in the areas mentioned above, many employers are beginning to turn to experienced workers aged fifty and older in order to gain and maintain a competitive edge.

Human resource managers who once may have assumed that older workers could be replaced by those fresh out of school are having to rethink those assumptions. Instead, many of them are now looking for innovative ways to encourage workers fifty and older to remain on the job beyond their traditional retirement age. They are learning that although these workers are motivated by current and future financial needs (e.g., pay and benefits), psychological and social fulfillment also play a significant role in decisions to keep working. As such, workers fifty and older highly value nonfinancial offerings by employers, such as flexible work schedules, telecommuting options, training and education opportunities, phased retirement programs, and bridge jobs that allow them to transition into some other kind of work.

Many employers have already begun implementing many of these innovative practices to attract and retain workers fifty and older. Others, however, are slow to adapt to the changing workforce, largely because of negative stereotypes and outdated notions about the value of older workers.

Despite the fact that more of us are choosing to remain in the workforce longer or to return to work in some capacity after having retired, either out of choice or financial necessity, many employers still see older workers as more of a liability than an asset and have yet to see the value older workers bring to their company's bottom line. They fail to accept the advantage gained by retaining, retraining, and recruiting older workers.

We need to challenge the outdated beliefs and stereotypes about older workers and create new solutions that provide all of us with more choices if we want or need to work beyond traditional retirement age.

Fighting the Stereotypes

One of the reasons many organizations can't see how workers fifty and older fit into today's fast-changing workplace is because they don't know who older workers are. Their perceptions of them are mired in past, outdated stereotypes that are just plain wrong. When we talk about older workers in this country the conversation usually begins with a negative predisposition of the problems older workers create for employers, with little regard for the benefits they bring. Older workers are presumed to cost more because they've been with the company longer and have higher healthcare costs, are less productive and less capable than younger workers, are more reluctant and slower to adapt to new technology, are more costly to train and resistant to change, and are less adaptable, innovative, creative, and willing to move if the job requires it.

Many of these beliefs and misperceptions are based on outdated stereotypes that fail to recognize the way people are aging today. For example, one misconception is that workers fifty and over cost significantly more than younger workers because of their experience and additional benefit costs. Although costs still tend to increase with age—particularly healthcare costs—the impact on the employer is minimal. In fact, recent trends in compensation and benefits have diminished the relationship between age and labor costs to the point that age is no longer a significant factor in the costs of hiring and retaining workers.

Likewise, research shows that worker productivity can increase with age, primarily as a result of experience and job tenure. People fifty and older are likely to be as or, in many cases, more productive than younger, less experienced workers. In fact, a University of Michigan study on the contributions older workers make to the economy and technological progress found that as the average age of the workforce increases, the overall workforce is more productive.

It's also a misperception that workers fifty and older are unable to learn or use new technology. The fact is that nine in ten regularly use a computer, tablet, or smartphone. Less than 20 percent feel like they have trouble keeping up with new technology required to do their jobs, and eight in ten are interested in taking training related to computers and information/communication technology. More often than not, the problems that workers fifty and older face when learning and using new technology are not because of age or that they can't learn it; instead, too many employers don't invest in training older workers. This issue is disappearing as computers and other digital devices become more pervasive in our lives and as the generation who grew up without computers exits the workforce.

Another misguided belief is that older workers are less innovative, creative, and adaptable than their younger colleagues. Workers with different backgrounds, experiences, and perspectives help create the kind of workplace where innovation can blossom. Experience tells us that organizations ruled by a hierarchy of imagination and innovation—and filled with people of all ages, races, and backgrounds—are the most successful. As discussed in Chapter 3, the late Dr. Gene Cohen found that creativity and innovation actually increase with age. And Vivek Wadhwa of the *Wall Street Journal* argues that "there is no age requirement for innovation, and we need both old and young working together." "The young," he says, "will dominate new-era software development, but the old will bring real-world and cross-disciplinary knowledge, management and business skills, and maturity. This is the combination we need to solve the big problems that the world faces."

There are two other reasons many employers are reluctant to retain, retrain, and recruit older workers, both based on outdated beliefs and perceptions. The first is that employers readily accept the "lump of labor" theory. This is the idea that if workers age fifty and over remain in the workforce, they will take opportunities away from younger workers and even push some out of the workforce. This theory has been around a long time and was long ago proven to be nonsense. It's based on the assumption that the number of jobs and the amount of wages in our economy is fixed when, in fact, both can expand or contract based on any number of economic factors. It's also mired in the outdated stereotype that older workers are not as productive as younger workers. As we challenge those stereotypes and emphasize the value older workers contribute to their employers, the "lump of labor" theory becomes less of an excuse for not employing and investing in older workers.

We heard this same argument as large numbers of women began entering the workforce in the second half of the twentieth century. Although there was some decrease in the number of males in the workforce, it was nowhere near the size of the increase in females working. And most of the decrease in male participation was among older workers, a decrease that has been attributed more to the availability of Social Security benefits and other pension and insurance systems than displacement.

Research shows, however, that when older people work, they spend more money, thus the economy grows, creating more jobs. Additionally, older workers also tend to give money to children and grandchildren, which they then spend or invest in the economy. Economists Jonathan Gruber and David Wise, who have studied this issue extensively, have found "no evidence that increasing the employment of older persons will reduce the employment opportunities of youth and no evidence that increasing the employment of older persons will increase the unemployment of youth."

The second reason is fear of intergenerational conflict. Nearly nine out of ten employers worry about hiring older workers because they fear that conflicts would arise when younger supervisors manage older workers.

Here's the rub: younger managers often don't know how to manage older workers—and older workers don't know how to get what they need from younger managers. Age is not the primary factor here; it has more to do with the difference in experience and the way in which younger managers try to supervise and motivate their more experienced workers. So not only do older workers need to continue to learn and keep their skills updated to remain valuable employees, but younger managers also need training programs aimed at teaching them how to work with older employees. Most employers motivate employees with money, promises of promotion and career advancement, and, in some cases, the fear of getting fired if they don't perform.

None of these factors matter as much to older workers, especially those who are near the end of their careers. Managing them requires a different approach. It begins with a different value proposition that includes giving greater importance to a sense of mission; serving a social purpose, which is something more than just making money for shareholders; offering flexibility in terms of work schedules; and offering a greater choice in benefits, including some targeted to older individuals.

Think of it this way: twenty-five years ago a key question among many male employees was, "Can I report to a woman?" Today that's a nonissue. Now the question among many older workers is, "Can I report to a younger person?" That's going to take some time to answer, but ultimately the answer will be, "Yes." It's happening more and more as the demographics continue to shift. But it requires change on the part of both younger managers and older workers. And if it's done right, it will lead to a better, stronger, and more productive workforce.

As workers aged fifty and older, we bring a lot of benefits to the workforce and add value in many different ways. We add value by exhibiting traits that are highly sought after in today's economy, including experience, maturity and professionalism, a strong work ethic, loyalty, reliability, knowledge and understanding, and the ability to serve as mentors. We are also more emotionally stable than our younger counterparts. We experience fewer negative emotions, are better at handling tense situations, are better collaborators, and have fewer conflicts than younger workers. Moreover, because we are less likely than younger workers to leave our jobs unexpectedly, we create value by allowing dollars and time that might otherwise be spent on workforce churn to be more effectively invested in productive measures that impact the bottom line. I find it particularly interesting that many employers won't hire or invest in someone who is older because they figure, *Why invest in an older person who is close to retirement and probably won't be around very long?* Yet millennials especially are known for jumping from one job to the next, not staying anywhere for more than a couple of years. It makes more sense to spend time and resources on an older worker who is more likely to stay rather than training an employee who in a year or two is likely to go to work for someone else, possibly a competitor.

We also create value through the impact we have on other employees. Research indicates that because older workers are highly engaged, motivated, and experienced, they help to create a more positive and effective work environment, which leads to increased productivity and business outcomes.

Our research at AARP found that most of us are still excited about our work. When we surveyed workers aged forty-five to seventy-four, the overwhelming majority said they are proud to work for their company, they are continuing to grow in their work, their job is an important part of who they are, and there is a lot they still plan to accomplish.

By focusing more on the positive aspects we bring to the workplace and challenging the outdated beliefs and stereotypes that permeate the conversations and perceptions of older workers, we can begin to spur solutions that create more choices for people who want or need to keep working past traditional retirement age. I believe that anyone who wants or needs to work should be able to work. It's not only essential to achieving financial security but also benefits our economy and society by allowing people to put their experience to work. People fifty and over bring huge economic benefits to employers as workers and as consumers, and when employers don't capitalize on that, they are doing themselves and their bottom line a huge disservice.

Creating Innovative Solutions for Putting Our Experience to Work

In years past, most individuals went through a fairly sequential pattern: education was for the young, work was for adults, and leisure or retirement was for the old. But that linear pattern has changed and no longer reflects the way many of us are living as we get older. More of us are working beyond traditional retirement age. We're also going back to school to learn new skills. Employers in many industries need older workers to keep working in order to meet projected employment gaps. So why do they persist in assuming older workers can no longer do the job? It's imperative that they adapt to accommodate older workers.

Adapting the Workplace to Accommodate Older Workers

When it comes to adapting the workplace to accommodate older workers, what older workers want is no different from what millennials and Gen Xers want: challenging, meaningful work; opportunities for learning, development, and advancement; support to successfully integrate work and personal life; fair treatment; and competitive compensation. And among the most important of all accommodations is flexibility. Flexibility is fundamentally about having control over the conditions of one's work and having the trust and respect of one's manager and employer. Research established these as key factors in motivation and commitment long before the invention of the smartphone. Employees across all generations value flexibility and view it as the key to helping employees balance the demands of work with those of life.

Flexible workplaces and job structures are about working differently in terms of when, where, and how work gets done. Flexibility can take a variety of different forms. It can include measuring results as opposed to the number of hours spent in the office; providing alternative work arrangements such as flex time, part time, telecommuting, compressed work weeks, and shift flexibility; and designing flexible work spaces with the assistance of technology. It can also include temporary assignments or contract arrangements.

When carmaker BMW looked at the demographics of its aging workforce, it decided to test the productivity and performance of assembly lines staffed by an older and a younger group of workers. It found that with minor adjustments in ergonomics, the productivity of the assembly line staffed with the older group rose to the same level as that of the lines staffed by the younger group, while absenteeism dropped below the plant average.

BMW made seventy small ergonomic design and equipment changes to accommodate older workers. These included new wooden floors, special barbershop-style chairs so employees could sit while working, installation of magnifying glasses to reduce eyestrain and mistakes, and daily stretching exercises, designed by a physiotherapist, to do while on the job.

Based on the success of the test, BMW implemented similar projects and equipment changes at plants around the world to help its current older workers and maintain or improve productivity.

CVS Caremark offers a different example of flexibility. It offers a "snowbird" program in which several hundred pharmacists and other employees from northern states are transferred each winter to pharmacies in Florida and other warmer states. This program not only appeals to older workers but also helps CVS keep up with the surge in business in the southern states it experiences during the colder months and creates training and mentorship opportunities while saving the company training and recruitment costs.

Home Depot hires thousands of older workers because it believes their experience gives the company a big advantage over its competitors. What it values most in older workers is their flexibility, which makes it easier for managers to fill weekly store schedules, and knowledge—many of them are so knowledgeable that they have become "associate coaches" to train and mentor younger workers.

In 2013 Susan Nordman, sixty, bought a struggling business, Erda, a small handbag company in Maine. Susan is committed to retaining her aging workforce by providing flexible hours so employees will stay long enough to pass their knowledge to more recent hires. She tells the *New York Times*, "Preserving critical knowledge is vital to the longevity of any business. The skills that my employees possess require hands-on learning. With time and training, new workers can learn these skills, but only if someone is there to teach them."

At Erda every employee has a key to the office, so workers can set their own schedules, sometimes opting to come in at 5:30 a.m. and taking a half day on Friday. Flexibility extends to employees' bodies too: Nordman offers a daily exercise session to keep her older staff nimble.

She also modernized the equipment to make it more ergonomic. The new equipment allows her workers to sit more of the time, rather than stand, and it reduces repetitive motion, which is a huge savings on joints.

Disproving stereotypes about older workers being slow to learn new ways of doing things, Ms. Nordman has found that learning has nothing to do with age. "My older workers embrace new methods quickly and easily," she said. "When I added a French seam to a design, we all gathered round the computer and watched a YouTube video to see how it was executed. The older staff picked it up immediately."

In addition to creating flexible workplaces and work structures, many employers are beginning to treat retirement as a process, not a single event. They are coming up with innovative ways of helping employees manage the transition to retirement or to some other kind of work. This includes a wide range of employment arrangements and accommodations that make it possible for an employee who is approaching traditional retirement age to continue working with a reduced workload and gradually transition from active, full-time employment to retirement. In some cases they also allow recently retired employees to transition back from retirement into a different temporary or project-based role.

Many of us say we expect or want to work later in life—and many are doing so—but we don't all want to work full time. We would like to have more time for nonwork activities while remaining actively employed, whether it's because we want to be physically or mentally engaged, we like contributing to society, or we simply enjoy what we're doing. That's why phased retirement, the gradual reduction of work with a long-term employer as an older employee approaches full retirement, is so appealing. Additionally many companies realize that they continue to need the expertise of their long-standing employees. Phased retirement is a way to ensure that older workers remain active and pass on knowledge of the organization. At AARP we have a "phased retirement" program that allows employees the opportunity to scale back their work as they ease into full retirement.

An approach that is gaining in acceptance is "retire and rehire." This allows employers to recall retired workers to return to work during peak times or on a temporary or project basis. The tire company Michelin North America, with more than twenty-two thousand employees, relies on its older workers for knowledge sharing, mentoring, and experience. They have established a formal Returning Retiree Employment program that allows former employees to return to Michelin on a reduced schedule if they want to continue working.

Beth Israel Deaconess Medical Center, a major teaching hospital of Harvard Medical School in Boston, Massachusetts, accepts many full-time, part-time, and per diem retirees back to work after a six-month termination of employment. In an industry where years of experience in various clinical disciplines has a direct impact on patient outcomes, they consider experienced older workers an invaluable asset for quality of care and informal mentoring.

Creating an Intergenerational Workforce

The aging of the workforce is having a disruptive influence in corporate America—and in the nonprofit sector as well. Businesses and organizations are struggling to find ways to manage their intergenerational workforces effectively. They're continually seeking ways of getting the most out of a workforce that may consist of up to four generations of workers—but most certainly has a larger proportion of older workers.

In a way the changes we face today in adapting to an older workforce are similar to those I encountered when I began my career in government over thirty years ago. At that time the issue was not how to deal with an influx of older workers but how to deal with the increasing number of women and minorities in the workforce. Embracing diversity has been a long and continuing journey for employers in all sectors across America. It has taught us the power of inclusion and that diversity is America's strength. The struggle today to embrace older workers is a continuation of that journey. Most corporate leaders today understand and accept the business advantage of a diverse workforce. But far fewer see older workers as part of that mix. Yet history tells us that organizations that fail to adapt to societal changes, including diversity and aging populations, risk stagnation that comes from being mired in the old way of doing things. A workplace with millennials, Gen Xers, baby boomers, and the Silent

Generation offers a unique opportunity for varied perspectives and approaches to day-to-day work.

GlaxoSmithKline, a global healthcare company, supports intergenerational understanding and cooperation through formal networking, mentoring programs, and cross-training opportunities. These programs give older workers an opportunity to feel connected to their younger colleagues, who in turn benefit from the older workers' knowledge and experience.

At Scripps Health, a private, nonprofit health system in San Diego, California, employees are invited to attend generation-specific, targeted educational programs. For example, they have programs for employees who are expectant parents, sessions for managing the challenges unique to sandwich generation employees who are juggling the needs of both children and aging parents, and sessions for employees who are caregivers.

Programs like these create a welcoming environment for older workers and younger workers, which in turn supports greater understanding among workers of all generations, thereby leading to greater engagement and commitment among all employees.

Creating New Opportunities

Even as people fifty and older are remaining in the workforce longer and more employers are looking at older workers to fill jobs in industries where shortfalls of trained workers are projected, older workers are not getting the training they need to fill those jobs and to remain relevant in the workplace. Older workers want the opportunity to use and expand their skills in order to remain productive and expand their career options, and they consider on-the-job training to be an important factor in determining whether they can do that. But there is a disconnect.

The overwhelming majority of training opportunities are provided to young workers in the early stages of their careers. Why, if older workers are being looked upon to contribute to the productivity of American business, aren't they being afforded opportunities for training and retraining to help them fulfill that role? The answer goes back to the old stereotypes and prejudices as well as a failure to recognize that the way people are aging today is markedly different from previous generations. To put it bluntly, many businesses are stuck in the old mindset and simply believe that training and retraining older workers is simply not worth the investment. Many believe that the older workers won't be around long enough for the company to recoup the investment, even though older workers are less likely to move than their younger counterparts. Additionally, as technologies change, many employers assume that older workers either don't want to learn, can't learn, or that it will take too long for them to become proficient in using new skills, while younger people are presumed to have more current skills and are more tech savvy. Research and experience shows that if the technology is good and works to help people do their jobs better, older people will readily learn it and embrace it if given the opportunity for training.

Access to training is also a key element of helping older workers continue their career growth and provides older workers with a path to transition into new roles that take advantage of their skills, expertise, and intelligence. When

I was at the Library of Congress as chief operating officer, we started a program of taking people—many of them the top expert curators in their field—and matching them with a technology expert, usually a younger employee. Dr. James H. Billington, the Librarian of Congress, called them "knowledge navigators." Through the use of technology, the historical materials, manuscripts, maps, and audio recordings that were once only available if you were visiting the Library of Congress in Washington, DC, could now be viewed and experienced in classrooms, libraries, and homes all over the world. The results of this program were staggering. For the curators, it showed them a whole new way to share their knowledge. The technology/digital experts gained much-needed experience in the content. And for the user, it made learning about history much more exciting. Many of the employees, most of whom were older and had spent many years at the library, told us they felt reinvigorated and saw their jobs in a whole new light. We retained many of our best employees, kept incredible talent from walking out the door, and provided many of our most experienced workers the opportunity to showcase their collections and their knowledge in a broader way.

Mentoring and Reverse Mentoring

Time and time again I've seen the benefit of older workers serving as mentors helping younger workers develop practical skills that can be learned on the job. Leveraging the skills and knowledge of older employees to transfer knowledge to younger workers and mentor them benefits the next generation as they take on new responsibilities.

Likewise entry-level employees who are fresh out of school can serve as reverse mentors by sharing the latest techniques, approaches, and theories with older workers. When I was leading AARP Foundation, we started a program called Mentor Up. This initiative engages young volunteers to teach older adults the basics on how to use and navigate the Internet using desktop computers, laptops, smartphones, and tablets. This program and others like it have been really taking off across the country.

The practice of pairing a tech-savvy twenty-something with an older executive is gaining popularity in the corporate world. The older partner gets a course in crafting a social media persona, while the younger receives lessons in business practice from an experienced professional. Ever since General Electric CEO Jack Welch championed the practice by requiring five hundred top-level executives to reach out to people below them to learn how to use the Internet, more and more executives have turned to reverse mentoring as a way to stay current. Sri Shivananda, vice president of global platform and infrastructure at PayPal, said it well: "I had adopted my learning from those who walked the path before me, but when it comes to learning about what's trending, the folks I needed for help were a completely different set of people," he says. "These are the younger members of the organization. They have the keys to trends and information I wasn't being exposed to."

Encore Careers

When Lester Strong was in the third grade, his teacher told his parents that they were wasting their time trying to give him a formal education. He was unteachable, destined for a life of manual labor. With a little luck, he might be able to live independently on his own someday, his teacher told them. To emphasize the point, Lester's teacher put his desk out in the hallway, away from the other students, to be on his own. One of eight children, Lester appeared to be one more unfortunate boy who would never get a chance to receive a quality education. His parents were overwhelmed, and his father had only an eighth-grade education. There wasn't a lot they could do.

Fortunately Lester had three mentors who told him he could learn, that he could succeed. They worked with him—checked his homework, looked over his report cards, and coached him on how to behave in school. Most important, they gave him hope and confidence and, in the process, transformed his life. Lester had to repeat third grade, but by fourth grade he had become an honors student and later graduated second in his high school class. He was selected as a National Merit Scholar, attended Davidson College on a scholarship, and then went on to Columbia Business School.

Lester went on to have a highly successful career in television, first as a reporter and then as an executive. He rose through the ranks to become the anchor of a daily newscast in Boston, where he was a fixture for many years.

But he never forgot his third-grade experience or the three mentors who turned his life around. "I felt the call to do something more meaningful," he says. "I wanted to give back by stopping children from being written off, as I almost was." So at age sixty Lester gave up the bright lights of being a television news anchor and began an encore career as chief executive of Experience Corps (now AARP Foundation Experience Corps), an organization that recruits volunteers over the age of fifty to mentor children from kindergarten through third grade, just as he was once mentored. Today AARP Experience Corps has more than two thousand volunteers aged fifty and older, working to improve the literacy of nearly thirty-two thousand inner-city school children in kindergarten through third grade in 211 schools across the country.

Lester's story is indicative of how the world of work is changing. An estimated 9 million Americans have followed Lester's path to pursue encore careers, and another 31 million are interested in doing so.

Encore careers, like Experience Corps, are the brainchild of Marc Freedman, CEO of Encore.org. An "encore career" is continued work in the second half of life that combines social impact, purpose, and, often, continued income. Marc sees encore careers as replacing the old goal of retirement, *freedom from work*, with a new one, *freedom to work*, that is more indicative of the way we are aging today.

As we disrupt aging, we're challenging the outdated beliefs and stereotypes about what it means to grow older and sparking new solutions so more people can choose how they want to age. That's what encore careers are all about. People like Lester who pursue encore careers are disruptors. They're challenging the old stereotypes, and through their work they're showing others what is possible by engaging in work that is not only personally meaningful but also has a positive impact on society.

The Gap Year

When my kids graduated from high school and college, some of their friends took a gap year to figure out what they wanted to do next. Now, as people enter extended middle age, more and more are taking a gap year to break out of their old routine, re-energize, and contemplate what they want to do next. Some people use this time to take a few classes, travel, attend life-planning workshops, volunteer, take on a big project, or just relax. Regardless of how they spend their time, they often find that the gap gives them a new perspective on their future, sometimes leading them to contemplate changes they had never considered before.

It's not all that uncommon for people to retire and then unretire a year or two later and return to work. In other words, they're using this period of retirement as a kind of gap year to think about what they want to do next.

The demographic changes we're experiencing with the aging of the population are creating opportunities for businesses and organizations to use the experience and wisdom that come with age and couple that with the digital literacy and imagination that youth brings. It's also an opportunity for older workers to think about how best to put their experience to work during their extended middle age.

We're beginning to see businesses and organizations with four generations working side by side in the workplace. This requires young and old to develop a culture of learning and respect for what each brings to the work experience. It requires us to develop solutions that support the new ways of work. We are beginning to create opportunities that capture the wisdom, knowledge, and experience of our older workforce and address the needs and desires of workers who are more likely to work from anywhere at any time. It's important to keep this trend going. We can find better ways to help employees transition into new careers without losing institutional knowledge. And we can find better ways to exchange knowledge and provide mentorship opportunities across generations of workers. We also need to foster new ways of working and engagement, like encore careers that empower people to pursue their purpose and passion for making a difference.

Finding solutions to these issues is important to all workers, not just older workers. As the Gen Xers and millennials move through their careers, the lines between work and retirement will become even more blurred. And as work becomes even more important as a way of financing our longer lives and remaining engaged as contributors to society, we need to expand the choices available to all of us who want or need to continue working.

Work as we know it is coming to an end. But as the growing number of people who are choosing to continue working beyond traditional retirement age remind us, that's not necessarily a bad thing. It could be that by disrupting work, we will put our experience to work and, then, discover the most meaningful work of our lives.

CHAPTER 8

Let's Change
the Rules

You never change things by fighting the existing reality.
To change something, build a new model that
makes the existing model obsolete.
—RICHARD BUCKMINSTER FULLER

In 2015 we celebrated the fiftieth anniversary of Medicare and Medicaid and the Older Americans Act, the eightieth anniversary of Social Security, and the fortieth anniversary of the Age Discrimination in Employment Act. These public policies and hundreds more like them were enacted during a time when not only life expectancy but also the experience of being older was much different from what it is today. For example, in 1935, when Social Security became law, life expectancy was sixty for men and sixty-four for women. Today it is seventy-six for men and eighty-one for women. Without question, public policies like Social Security, Medicare, Medicaid, and others have played an important role in helping people live longer and better.

We have made adjustments to policies and practices to help us age better over the years, and we have updated the infrastructure that supports us as we age, but the truth is, our programs, institutions, and policies—and, in a sense, our culture—have not kept up with the way people are aging today. Most of them were designed for a twentieth-century lifestyle and don't adequately support the way we live today.

As the baby boomers age—the first ones are now turning seventy—our infrastructure and systems for supporting people as they age are becoming more and more outdated. So just as the *birth* of the boomers caused a disruption of our culture and social institutions, the *aging* of the boomers requires similar disruption.

As we've seen in the previous chapters, many of us are already disrupting aging in our personal lives as we seek to figure out how we want to live as we age, gain more control over our health, and make our financial resources last. I've talked about the changes that we need to make in how we approach health, how we adapt our communities, and how we envision work and retirement. In this chapter I want to explore some of the rules, policies, programs, and institutions that we are endeavoring to change in order to support us as we prepare for and live longer lives. Although the list is not exhaustive, it does represent AARP's most important priorities. I hope it will also spark new ideas in you to find solutions that update and adapt our infrastructure to support us as we live and age in the twenty-first century.

Health

As we transform health from a focus on treating disease to helping us achieve health and well-being, we need to have policies, practices, and institutions that align to ensure that people fifty and older have access to the care, information, and services they need to lead healthier lives.

Healthy Living

Our current healthcare system can better be described as a "sick care" system. If you can afford it, it's good at treating you once something is wrong with you, but it does very little to help keep you healthy. Although we're starting to see some positive developments that are contributing to a greater focus on health and wellness—for example, the Affordable Care Act includes a provision that focuses on prevention, and Medicare now offers a free "Welcome to Medicare" physical for all new Medicare patients—this is only the beginning, and we need to do much more. We at AARP have been on the front lines of this battle and have identified key areas that need attention.

We have to make the entire system work more efficiently. As consumers, we have a role to play in this, but much of the responsibility lies with providers, payers, and policymakers. We can lower costs by improving health outcomes, not by shifting costs to patients and consumers. Likewise we need to continue to develop new delivery models. For most of us, health care is uncoordinated, quality is uneven, and the cost is increasingly unaffordable. The most common way we pay physicians—fee for service—encourages this fragmented delivery. It offers clinicians and health plans little incentive to improve, coordinate, or integrate care to make it more efficient.

The Patient Protection and Affordable Care Act (ACA) includes several provisions to address these affordability and quality concerns. For example, the new Center for Medicare & Medicaid Innovation will test payment and service delivery models that reduce spending while enhancing quality care. The Center will give preference to programs that improve the coordination, quality, and efficiency of patient-centered health care. It will also promote broad payment and practice reforms. Other provisions authorize pilot-testing of new care models such as medical homes and accountable care organizations.

We need to continue this work and explore new incentives for providers and new thinking by a wide range of healthcare stakeholders. These include innovative solutions such as expanding payment innovations to promote value not volume, promoting greater care coordination (e.g., making sure all of our doctors and practitioners are talking to each other), implementing measures to lower drug costs, providing consumers with better information on cost and quality of services, and working to make healthcare programs more efficient and less wasteful. These steps will bring significant savings, spur innovative cost reductions in private insurance, and, most importantly, help people to get and stay healthier.

We will all benefit if these kinds of innovative approaches and other reforms improve the quality of care we receive and make it more affordable. It may seem counterintuitive as a healthcare "innovation," but one way we can do this is by going back to the practice of home doctor visits for the oldest and frailest. According to a study by Medstar Health in the Washington, DC, area, this "innovation" has demonstrated a potential 17 percent cost savings for Medicare among the oldest of the population.

One good way to improve efficiency is to create more transparency throughout the healthcare system. In fact, this is essential for improving the healthcare system. That burden lies mostly with major stakeholders—hospitals and doctors, insurance companies, and politicians. But it will only happen if we as consumers demand it. As healthcare consumers, we often don't have the information we need to make rational decisions and seek value. Transparency, fair prices, known quality—factors we take for granted in other markets—are often not available in the healthcare marketplace. We already shoulder an increasing financial burden for health care, and we are at the mercy of our doctors, hospitals, insurance companies, and a complex system of rules, regulations, and practices that we often do not understand and have no ability to change. We need to demand more transparency and information from our practitioners and tell our leaders to pass laws and implement regulations to make the healthcare system more transparent and consumer friendly.

Medicare

Millions of older Americans depend on Medicare for guaranteed, affordable health coverage. In 2014 Medicare provided health insurance coverage to 53.8 million people. Total Medicare expenditures were $613 billion, and income was $599 billion. The average Medicare benefit per enrollee was $12,179. By 2020 64 million Americans are expected to be enrolled in Medicare. Yet the latest Medicare Trustees report shows that Medicare will remain solvent until 2030, demonstrating the ongoing financial challenges facing Medicare along with the overall high cost of health care. Because so many of us rely and will rely on Medicare as our primary means to pay for health care, it is imperative that we address its long-term solvency and take appropriate steps to update it to support the way we are aging today and in the future.

We can reduce costs and find significant savings in Medicare using responsible solutions rather than applying harmful cuts to beneficiaries in an attempt to save money. Policymakers seeking to reduce or slow the rising cost of Medicare often see only two options: either reduce the amount of services or pass the costs on to the consumer. Either way, we end up paying. But there are other things we can do to make Medicare more efficient and less expensive. First, we can improve the coordination of care. Most of us today don't just see one doctor but rather have a primary doctor as well as any number of specialists. But let's face it: these doctors don't do a very good job of talking to each other, and it's often left up to us to coordinate our own care. With the technology we have today there's no reason our care can't be better coordinated. This would go a long way in avoiding duplication of tests and lab work, using medical technology more efficiently, and reducing unnecessary procedures and services. Medicare costs can also be reduced by addressing skyrocketing drug prices and continuing to ferret out fraud and abuse. All of these steps will improve our healthcare system as a whole while at the same time will save money in Medicare.

Family Caregivers

Today about 40 million Americans care for older parents, spouses, or other loved ones who need help with everyday activities and tasks, even medical and nursing tasks. These can include housekeeping, means, personal care like bathing or getting dressed, scheduling appointments, personal finances, medication management, wound care, and transportation. We estimate the economic value of their unpaid contributions at roughly $470 billion a year. If they were no longer available to provide such care, the economic costs to our public support systems would skyrocket. That's why it's critical we develop policies and a nationwide strategy and infrastructure to recognize and support family caregivers.

Several policy options are being introduced and implemented in the states to address family caregiving issues. For example, the CARE Act (Caregiver, Advise, Record, Enable Act) supports family caregivers when their loved ones go into the hospital and when they transition home. Financial caregiving legislation helps family caregivers navigate financial challenges. These include bills such as the Uniform Adult Guardianship and Protect Proceedings Jurisdiction Act, which ensures adult guardianship laws are consistent and honored from state to state. The Uniform Power of Attorney Act does the same thing for power-of-attorney laws. Some states have also introduced a modest caregiver tax credit that gives family caregivers some relief when they use their own money to care for a loved one. AARP's Caregiving Resource Center (www.aarp.org/home-family/caregiving) provides information on caregiving policies and resources available in each state.

Some states have significantly increased the number of older adults who have access to state-funded services at home, such as home care and adult day services. Similarly many states have increased funding for respite care services that allow family caregivers to take a hard-earned break. Legislative proposals have been introduced to cut through the red tape and allow advanced practice nurses to serve as the primary or acute care provider of record and to allow nurses to delegate tasks such as giving medication to trained home care workers in regular direct contact with consumers.

Other legislative proposals address the issue of workplace flexibility to help working caregivers balance responsibilities at home and work through state improvements to the Federal Family and Medical Leave Act or to employers' paid or unpaid leave policies.

Some employers have made changes to support caregivers through their involvement in ReACT (Respect A Caregiver's Time), an employer coalition dedicated to addressing the challenges employee caregivers face and reducing the impact on the companies that employ them. ReACT represents nearly 1 million employees through its membership of more than thirty companies and nonprofit organizations.

The Healthcare Workforce

We can't expect families to shoulder the entire responsibility of caring for our aging population. In fact, we face a growing care gap: the number of available family caregivers is declining and unlikely to keep pace with future demand. Rapidly

increasing numbers of people in advanced old age and with shrinking families to provide support to them demand that we come up with new solutions. The past suggests that families will continue as the backbone of support for older loved ones, but the future suggests that family caregivers themselves will require more support to meet the increased stress and burdens that are certain to occur.

We need millions of workers with a broad range of skills and training. We need more geriatricians, nurses, psychologists, social workers, pharmacists, physical therapists, care coordinators, and home health aides. And we need teachers to educate and train all of these workers as well as more young people who seek these kinds of jobs, which can often be very demanding and very low pay.

Direct-care workers—such as home health aides, personal-care attendants, and certified nursing assistants—are also in short supply. Direct-care workers provide most paid services and supports, but people with self-care needs and their family caregivers often cannot locate the right people to do the job. Low wages and few benefits add to the high staff turnover and low quality of care.

One important way to address this problem is to broaden the scope of responsibilities to help attract and retain workers. Finding ways for all professionals to provide services to the full extent of their training, experience, and skill level would go a long way toward easing access-to-care caused by personnel shortages. Establishing worker registries would also help consumers find direct-care workers. And as we saw in Chapter 4, technology entrepreneurs are coming up with innovative online approaches to matching workers with caregiver needs.

Wealth

Having the financial resources and opportunities to match our longer lives is a tremendous challenge that requires public policies and private-sector practices to be aligned, working in support of individuals. We devoted Chapter 7 to work and workforce issues that merit disruption, but there are other policies and practices that need to change as well.

Social Security

Ever since Ida Mae Fuller received the first Social Security check in January 1940, Social Security has helped people live their lives with independence and dignity. For generations Social Security has been the bedrock of a secure retirement for millions of Americans who pay in over a lifetime of hard work. It also has provided critical protection for younger families when a worker dies or suffers a disability. Its importance cannot be overstated: Social Security represents a sacred trust that Americans depend on. In 2013 Social Security kept over 22 million Americans of all ages out of poverty.

Two-thirds of Americans across demographic and political lines say Social Security is one of the most important government programs, and nearly nine in ten adults under thirty want to know it will be there when they retire.

The 2015 Social Security Trustees Report found that the combined old age, survivor and disability insurance trust funds can pay full retirement, survivor, and disability benefits for approximately two more decades, and between 73 and 79 percent after that. If no action is taken to address

Social Security's long-term shortfall, benefits will be cut by more than 20 percent in 2034. So we need to make sure Social Security is sufficiently financed to ensure solvency for the long term while continuing to provide adequate benefits for future generations.

As we consider the future of Social Security, we must do so in the context of how society is changing—not just how to make it solvent and adequate in the near term but how to make it better for the long term. Although the current program has been a great success, it requires updating to address demographic and economic changes over the last eighty years and respond to the needs of future beneficiaries and their families.

Social Security was created at a much different time in our history, when most women didn't work outside the home and life expectancy at birth was around sixty. But that's not the case today. Aging today is different from what it was even a generation ago, and it will be different for generations into the future. Women are working outside the home more than ever, but the system was set up at a time when the single-breadwinner couple was the norm. We no longer live our lives in a linear progression from education to work to retirement. We move in and out of these phases throughout our lives. As more of us are living into our eighties, nineties, and beyond, benefits are often inadequate for the oldest beneficiaries.

We need to update Social Security to meet these changing realities. In figuring out how to do that, we need to keep what works, make changes and improvements where needed, and take the steps to achieve long-term financial stability. This is a complex issue that cannot be solved by simply raising the retirement age or reducing benefits, as some politicians would have us believe. It involves much more than that. And as our political leaders figure out how best to solve it, we need to encourage them to be guided by some very basic principles.

First, Social Security should be *sufficiently financed to ensure solvency and meaningful benefits* for the long term. Second, we need to *reaffirm Social Security's fundamental character.* If we seek a future in which all workers and families can live with financial security and stability after experiencing major life events such as retirement, disability, or the death of a loved one, then Social Security must include all workers and ask workers to contribute equitably. All workers should have a stake in the program. All should pay in, and all should be protected. The partnership among individuals, employers, and the federal government is critically important and must endure.

Third, it should *ensure protections for those most in need* by taking into account the needs of those most reliant on Social Security and those who have difficulty postponing retirement. Although Social Security protects virtually all workers, it can do more to support the most vulnerable. This includes many women because they tend to live longer than men, earn less, and take time out of the workforce for caregiving or to raise children.

Fourth, reforms should *recognize the value of Social Security's core elements by retaining the features that have made it such a strong foundation of retirement security.* Even though Social Security faces financial challenges down the road, workers and their families will still depend on the program's core elements. Workers must continue to earn Social Security benefits that provide a solid foundation of retirement income, protect them against inflation, protect them and their families if they get hurt or sick and can no longer work, and protect their family members in case of early death. Social Security should continue to reward work. It must continue to protect people from economic volatility and offer benefits that are predictable, stable, and last a lifetime. The key elements of Social Security's successful program structure should be preserved: progressive, defined benefits that cannot be outlived; inflation protection; and benefits related to earnings.

Fifth, improvements should reflect *today's workforce*. The changing economy has added to the financial challenge of many workers and of Social Security itself. For hard-working Americans the dream of a secure retirement is increasingly elusive. Most workers are finding it harder or even impossible to get ahead. As wages have stagnated, saving for retirement has become more difficult. The rise in income inequality has weakened Social Security's financial position, as a growing share of earnings in the economy is not taxed for Social Security purposes. Social Security must respond to these new realities. An updated Social Security program must address the economic and demographic changes over the last eighty years to be able to respond to the needs of future beneficiaries and their families. Also, a twenty-first-century program of Social Security should be more user-friendly. Administrative reforms can increase efficiency, promote transparency, and make it easier for people to understand how and when to collect the benefits they have earned.

Finally, as updates are made to Social Security, they must *ensure fairness*. Changes to the program should be implemented gradually and should protect current beneficiaries and near retirees. We have to figure out how to make sure that those who have paid into and earned Social Security benefits receive them. Current beneficiaries must know that the benefits they rely on every day will not be reduced or taken away, and those nearing eligibility must know that the promise of benefits based on what they have paid into the program will be kept. At the same time, young people and future generations should be secure in the knowledge that their contributions bring meaningful protections and that they can live in dignity when they get older.

Work and Save

Although updating Social Security is critical to having enough money to live on as we get older, it was never meant to be anyone's sole source of retirement income (though for many it is). We have to find ways to encourage and help more people save more for their later years. The fact is that almost half of all people over age fifty-five have saved less than $50,000. No wonder so many people worry that they will outlive their money.

Many younger people don't save. They either can't afford to or think they can't afford to. But the real problem is that our current policies and practices don't encourage or make it easy for those who can save even just a small amount each month to do so. Fifty-five million Americans have no access to a retirement savings plan through their employers—that's about half of the eighteen- to sixty-four-year-old population—and of those who do, too many don't participate. More than half of all private-sector employers don't even offer a savings plan to their employees, but when employers give workers the option of payroll deduction for retirement savings, their participation rate is a whopping success.

Employers could do a lot more to make it easier for people to save. Most employers who offer 401(k) plans or other retirement savings vehicles require employees to opt in to the plan. But behavioral science has shown that plans with automatic enrollment increase employee participation, and those with auto-escalation of contributions (e.g., every time you get a raise, your contribution to your retirement savings plan also increases) help people save more over time. So simply by using automatic enrollment, employers can help their employees save more and make it easier for them to do so.

We also need to consider public policy proposals to promote workplace savings. More than twenty states are offering or considering offering state-sponsored retirement savings plans for small business employees known as Work and Save plans, or Automatic IRAs. These plans make it easier for businesses to create a private retirement savings account for employees, helping them take charge of their financial futures and live independently as they age. They are easy to set up and involve no ongoing costs or risks to the employers or the state.

Work and Save plans also make it easier for employees to save more so they can live a secure and independent future. Accounts are voluntary; it's up to employees to decide whether they want to participate. Accounts are also portable: when employees switch jobs they often can take their Work and Save accounts with them.

Another way we can encourage people to save is by reforming our tax code to expand incentives for lower-income workers by providing a more generous or refundable Saver's Credit (which is currently capped at $1,000 per individual). The Saver's Credit gives a special tax break to low- and moderate-income taxpayers who are saving for retirement, and expanding incentives would go a long way to help low-income workers build up a nest egg for the future.

As a society we also have to do a lot more to raise public awareness that saving matters—it's not something we can put off. We need to get the message out that people should start saving early and avoid withdrawing the money before retirement if at all possible. Employees who participate in employer-sponsored retirement savings plans or state-based Work and Save plans need to stay in those plans throughout their working lives to allow their nest egg to grow. Giving employees a simple way to save for retirement also means fewer Americans will need to rely on government safety net services, which will save taxpayer dollars.

Managing and Protecting Your Nest Egg

Building a retirement nest egg is only part of the answer. We also need new and better solutions to help manage and protect them. Since the demise of defined benefit pension plans, most of the responsibility for building and managing retirement savings has shifted to us as individuals, but that doesn't mean we have to go it alone.

Having the capability to manage our finances in an increasingly complex world is more important today than ever. Yet financial incompetence is widespread among all segments of our society and all income levels, especially students, women, people with low incomes, and, surprisingly, those over fifty. Too often we see the evidence—higher levels of debt, less saving, and too little retirement planning. In short, a lack of financial know-how is a major barrier to achieving financial security in retirement.

We cannot improve money management skills simply by directing financial education at the fifty-and-over population. To achieve financial security later in life one must begin early in life. So we must address the problem of financial literacy with youth in our schools, with employees in the workplace, and with families in our communities.

Unfortunately most of us think we know a lot more about personal finance than we actually do. Half of all workers have no sense of how much they will need to save for retirement. According to the Center for Retirement Research at Boston College, almost 44 percent of working-age households (ages thirty-six to sixty-two) are "at risk" of having insufficient savings for their retirement years. This puts even greater pressure on national retirement systems that already face solvency challenges.

By adopting "smart" auto-features in savings plan designs, such as auto-enrollment, auto-escalation, and automatic rebalancing, employers can provide their employees with financial resources and tools to help them save and prepare financially. Additionally a wide array of online resources and decision-making tools such as retirement calculators, Social Security calculators and long-term-care calculators can help us navigate the increasingly complex financial landscape.

Americans should also learn, practice, and share the core concepts of prudent financial management with their families and in their communities. Research shows that parents are the single-greatest influencers of positive financial attitudes and behaviors in their children. We also need to develop new and innovative ways to help vulnerable older workers and job seekers in the communities where they live by teaching them how to set goals and implement action plans to reduce debt, repair credit, build savings, and regain control of their finances.

Having the financial capability to manage our money is an essential part of constructing a solid foundation for individuals' financial resilience as well as economic growth and prosperity for the nation. More of us are turning to financial advisers for professional advice—where to invest, when to change investments, when to withdraw money, how much, what are the risks and trade-offs. Although many financial advisers work hard to help us protect and grow our savings, some don't. Loopholes in the law allow many financial advisers to offer advice based on what's best for them, not for the person saving for retirement. We need to change that. In today's world it's hard enough to save for retirement and achieve our financial goals; we don't need to make it more difficult by allowing some in the financial industry to take advantage of us. All advice should be in the best interest of the consumer. We deserve investment advice based on what's truly best for us and our financial future. And we need a standard that holds all of Wall Street genuinely accountable for helping us choose the best investments for ourselves and our futures.

Another challenge most of us face is how to convert our savings into a steady stream of lifetime income. Many financial advisers say the answer is to buy an annuity. This removes the risks of longevity, fluctuating interest rates and inflation while providing a steady monthly income for a set period of time. But we know that very few people (only about 6 percent of households) have income from private annuities. They can also be complicated and expensive. When interest rates are as low as they are today, it takes a lot of money to produce a moderate stream of income, and few employers offer them as a payout option. On top of that, many people are reluctant to turn over their life savings to invest in an annuity.

Having said that, annuities could help provide an important lifetime income option as we get older. And the financial services industry is developing new lifetime income products to address these concerns. For example, because many people don't understand how annuities work, some companies are now offering the option of purchasing a life annuity for a trial period, perhaps two years, to help people become more familiar with them. At the end of the two-year trial period the purchaser would have the option of either continuing the annuity or receiving a lump-sum payment. Another innovative approach is to encourage the gradual annuitization of contributions to 401(k) and other direct contribution plans made over the course of a plan member's working life. Under this approach we no longer face the decision of converting a large balance into an annuity at the end of our career with only one or a few payments. The financial industry needs to continue to create new solutions that provide more lifetime income options that address our financial needs as we get older and help ensure that we don't outlive our money.

We need to change the rules that govern and guide how we manage and protect our earnings. We can't afford to work hard all our lives to accumulate savings for our future only to see that money disappear because of loopholes in the laws that are designed to help us protect and manage our retirement nest egg.

Age-Friendly Banking

Financial institutions play a critical role throughout our lives, but as we get older our relationship with our bank and investment advisors begins to change. As we focus more on our own financial future, our desire to be financially secure, and our fear of outliving our money, we need to have confidence that our assets will not be lost to fraud and exploitation. We need to be able to access the services we depend on and conduct our business securely. We need to be able to make informed decisions for ourselves and to choose responsible financial caregivers before we need them. Age-friendly banking is a way to address all those needs that benefit not only individuals but financial institutions as well.

The first principle of age-friendly banking is to prevent financial exploitation and fraud aimed at older consumers. This is a growing problem as those of us in the boomer generation age and people live longer. Consumers over fifty own the majority of America's financial assets, and financial exploitation is the fastest-growing form of elder abuse.

Secondly, we can do more to empower older consumers, including people with dementia who rely on financial caregivers. Existing tools are helping, but we need to go farther. Bank employees need greater training and awareness. The growing prevalence of cognitive impairment adds to the challenge. We need more strategies to help financial care-givers, who do a very difficult job.

A third principle of age-friendly banking is to make the bank environment easier to access and navigate. It should be easy, whether you are physically going to the bank or connecting digitally through your computer, smartphone, or tablet. Just think of the challenges for someone who has issues with vision, hearing, mobility, or cognitive function. For example, written and online statements should be easy to see and read, and mobile or remote access should be safe and secure without being complicated.

And finally, age-friendly banking encourages older house-holds' financial stability and helps safeguard their assets. Nearly 17 million Americans aged forty-five and over live in households that are financially underserved. They may rely on services like payday lending rather than routine banking. This underserved group would prefer to use banks for their basic financial needs and, thus, represent a market opportu-nity for banks and credit unions.

Creating more age-friendly banking will require a wide range of expertise incorporating insights from the finance and banking world and aging consumers as well as aging advocate groups. We need to highlight existing tools and services that can serve the people fifty and older and their families as well as develop new innovations to help them even more. For example, Barclays developed a training pro-gram called the Community Driving License that teaches all of their employees how to interact better with vulnera-ble customers. Employees receive online training on fraud and exploitation, dementia, vulnerabilities, and accessibil-ity. Barclays also uses data analytics to identify customers at risk of fraud and exploitation and is now testing how to provide education to protect those customers.

We also need to enhance bank employee training to fight fraud and, even more broadly, to foster a friendly banking culture for older consumers. Bank of American Fork promotes an age-friendly culture by having "age-friendly champions" at each of its branches. These champions receive extra training on how to spot fraud or a stressed caregiver and are a source of information and support for employees in addressing the needs of older adults. They have also implemented age-friendly products and features such as third-party monitoring to a checking account, power-of-attorney, automatic bill pay, and payable-upon-death accounts. This third-party monitoring, also known as Read Only, authorizes a family member or friend to monitor an older adult's account for irregularities but does not provide access to funds or the ability to make transactions.

Finally, we need to do more to educate consumers about fraud and exploitation, including special guidance and support for financial caregivers. The Oregon Bankers Association developed a training kit aimed at preventing elder fraud and exploitation. Every bank in Oregon as well as banking associations in every state has received the kit. As a result of this outreach and training, banks in Oregon are now the second-largest reporter of elder abuse in the state.

Age-friendly banking is a way to address many of the financial needs and concerns of people aged fifty and over at the point when they need expert support—when they are making financial decisions and using financial services. People aged fifty and over are a large segment of financial institutions' customer base, and they have unique and changing banking needs, including fraud protection, knowledgeable financial caregivers, and accessibility. By addressing these needs, financial institutions not only gain customer trust and loyalty; they also protect themselves from losses due to fraud and financial exploitation against their customers.

Self

As we grow older, most of us want to continue to be regarded as an integral and inspirational asset to society. We're focused more on living than we are on aging. We still have goals and dreams, and we're determined to find and fulfill our purpose in life. But as we strive to pursue our own idea of personal fulfillment, we're often met with barriers that either keep us from doing what we want to do or make it extremely difficult. Some of these are cultural, some are behavioral, and some are institutional. Part of disrupting aging is fighting through these barriers and changing institutions that get in our way so we can choose the way we want to live and age.

Ageism

Ageism is one of the last frontiers of discrimination. We don't accept discrimination for race, gender, sexual preference, or financial status, but we allow ageist thinking to go on for people fifty and older. When are we going to stop that? Institutional ageism is the major barrier to our full participation in society. We represent an enormous source of civic and economic growth, but because of ageist attitudes and assumptions about our abilities and usefulness, we often don't get the opportunity to contribute. We have to confront individual acts of ageism, but we also have to make it clear that there is no place in our society for institutional ageism.

Opportunities for Civic and Social Contributions

Our increased longevity and generally better health has opened our eyes to new and increased opportunities to contribute to the betterment of society through civic, social, and economic engagement in activities we believe in. These can range from mentoring to volunteering, to second and third careers, to continuing education. The question is: How do we design and implement policies and break down institutional barriers so we can make these contributions? That's our challenge. It's not just about creating more volunteer opportunities; it's about creating a new infrastructure for supporting the civic, social, and economic contributions of people fifty and over and weaving that into the social fabric of our culture. One place we're beginning to see this happen is in the workplace. Not only are we seeing more and more employers offering employee volunteer programs, many who once viewed them as a nice thing to do now see them as essential to their business. These employer-sponsored programs provide service opportunities for employees to put their passions, skills, and talents to work for the good of the community. At AARP, for example, we offer a Community Builders program that allows employees forty-eight hours per year paid time to pursue volunteer service. According to the nonprofit LinkedIn for Good, over 4 million professionals have actively signaled on their LinkedIn profiles that they are interested in volunteering.

Education

We're all too familiar with the old adage "live and learn." For those of us fifty and older, the phrase takes on new meaning. Boomers in particular are going back to school. Some want to learn new skills or update old ones. Some are using their considerable experience to teach others. Others are going back to take a course they find personally interesting or enriching. And many are going back to get help figuring out how to handle the transition from middle age to a new extended middle age. They're searching for their sense of purpose and trying to develop strategies for moving forward. They're looking for life skills to help them handle life's transitions.

Colleges and universities have been slow to catch on, and community colleges much less so. Like so many of our institutions, the college and university system was designed at a time when life expectancy was about half of what it is today. But think about it: given what life expectancy is today, if we were designing a new system of educational institutions, would we design those institutions primarily to serve an age group of eighteen- to twenty-two-year-olds? Or would we design it to serve a broader population throughout the course of their lives? Our colleges and universities need to broaden their horizons and think about what they have to offer the growing population of people fifty and over who have a burning desire to keep learning.

One way they are doing this is through the development of Massive Open Online Courses, or MOOCs. As the name suggests, MOOCs are available online and offer unlimited participation. They are highly flexible and can be taken for college credit or certification or just for the sake of learning. In addition to traditional course materials, such as filmed lectures, required and suggested readings, and other types of learning exercises, they also offer interactive discussion groups. Some students will create community discussion groups by identifying others in their community who are taking the course, and they will often gather in local coffee shops or libraries to discuss the lectures, reading assignments, and course materials. MOOCs have gained popularity among people fifty and older who just want to learn for fun or who are going back to school. Their flexibility makes them an attractive way to continue learning and to stay engaged.

Environment

If our environment doesn't fit, we need to adapt our public policies and practices to make it fit. Think, for example, about transportation. Most of our public transportation systems are designed to move commuters to and from work. If you want to take a city bus to go to the grocery store or the doctor in the middle of the afternoon, good luck. You may be in for a two-hour tour of the city just to go a few miles.

Pedestrian fatalities alone accounted for 14 percent of all deaths on America's roadways in 2011, and nearly one in five of those deaths was a person sixty-five or older. Sadly every two hours a pedestrian is killed because of unsafe streets or crosswalks.

To combat this problem, more than seven hundred jurisdictions throughout the country have adopted safe streets policies (as with the New York City example I mentioned in Chapter 5). Over half of these are in small cities and rural areas. These policies are sometimes called "complete streets" because they require planners to take all users—pedestrians, bicyclists, bus riders, and motorists—into account when designing new roads or fixing existing ones. Research shows that well-designed intersections, sidewalks, bike lanes, extended pedestrian crossing times, countdown traffic signals, and other features can significantly reduce injuries, deaths, and automobile crashes. Yet despite these efforts, too many people cannot safely walk, bike, or take public transportation to their destinations.

As we think about how we are aging today, we have to realize that many of our institutions, social structures, and, in fact, our culture were just not designed to support an aging society. We need to re-engineer many aspects of our society—health care, work and retirement, education, transportation, urban planning, housing, and community development—if we're going to thrive and grow and contribute as we get older. We must become advocates for making change happen. We need to change the rules.

We all have a role to play in this. Dr. Ethel Percy Andrus founded AARP on the principles of collective voice, collective purpose, and collective purchasing power. And those principles still ring true today. Those of us fifty and over are a powerful force for change. In this chapter I've discussed some of the important changes we need to make. By and large we know what needs to be done. The question is: Do we have the will to make it happen? In our younger years we came together with a collective voice, collective purpose, and collective purchasing power to change America's public policies, social institutions, attitudes, and culture. Now we need to do it again to change our public policies, social institutions, attitudes, and culture around the issues we face as our society grows older. We need to make our voices heard— in Washington, in our state capitals, in our communities. We need to be the change we want to see happen—by the way we live, speak out, and engage others. We have tremendous opportunities in front of us. If we come together to create the societal change we know we need and then combine that with the knowledge, innovation, technology, and wisdom that comes from having lived, we can grasp those opportunities and create an America where all people can age with independence, dignity, and purpose.

To me it comes down to this: we can join together in a movement to disrupt aging by challenging outdated beliefs and attitudes, updating public policies and social institutions, and creating new solutions so we can choose how we want to age, or we can let aging disrupt us by forcing us to adapt to and live in a world that no longer fits our wants and needs, makes us feel like outsiders, and doesn't allow us to continue to grow and contribute and fulfill our purpose in life. Our choice is clear.

A New Vision for Living and Aging in America

You can never plan the future by the past.
—EDMUND BURKE

I first stepped onto the stage at AARP's Ideas@50+ national member event in San Diego in September 2014 to deliver a keynote address urging the eight thousand attendees to disrupt aging. Since then the response has been overwhelming. It turns out that this is a message people aged fifty and over have been waiting to hear. People across the country, from all walks of life, have been sharing their experiences with me and telling me that although they don't want to age the same way their parents did, they aren't sure what to do about it. They are anxious to change the conversation in our society and, in some cases, to start *having* the conversation. They want more choices for how to live when they get older. They want new and better solutions to help them age with independence, dignity, and purpose. They are ready to chart a new course. So am I.

I wrote this book to provide a pathway for those who are fifty and over and to create a new vision for all generations for living and aging in America. I can no more identify with my parents' experience of aging than my own kids can identify with mine—it's just different. Sometimes I play this little game when I hit certain milestones in my life, like birthdays, sending my kids off to college, attending their graduations, and so forth. I think back and try to remember my parents as they experienced those same milestones. What was my mom like when she was fifty-seven? What were my parents doing when I graduated from college? How did they view their lives at various milestones along the way? It can be a real eye opener and really makes me realize how much things have changed from their generation to mine.

The way we are aging today is dramatically different from how it was a generation, even a decade ago. Yes, we are living longer and in better health, but it's much more than that. We haven't just added more years to the end of life; we've extended middle age and, in essence, created a new life stage that has opened up a whole new world of possibilities for how we live and age. And we're just beginning to understand the full range and depth of those possibilities. We live today during a time when people age sixty and over outnumber children fifteen and under. Demographers predict that more than half the children born today will live to 100. And some believe that the first person who will live to the age of 150 has already been born.

This is an incredibly exciting time. Many organizations and companies that five or ten years ago had no interest in aging issues and didn't even want to acknowledge aging are now engaging and becoming part of the broadening conversation. Ten years ago we had to practically beg celebrities to appear on the cover of *AARP: The Magazine.* Now we are approached constantly by stars who want to be on the cover. Entrepreneurs and innovators are creating an incredible array of products and services targeted to people fifty and older. Advances in research and technology are driving innovation in virtually every field of endeavor that affects our ability to live well as we age. Science is making longer lives possible. Now we have to figure out what we're going to do with them.

Even as all of these exciting developments are changing the way we age, most conversations around aging still view it as a problem to be solved. And the solutions are all an effort to avoid the national crisis that is the aging of America. It's a premise that is absolutely and fundamentally wrong, and millions of people are proving it wrong every day. The conversation can't be about how to avoid a crisis; it needs to be about how to take advantage of the opportunities we have so we, individually and as a nation, can thrive.

Our culture, institutions, social supports, and infrastructure have not kept up with the advancements in the way we age that science, technology, and innovation have made and continue to make possible. That's what the conversation is about. We need to get rid of the outdated beliefs and stereotypes about aging and spur new solutions so more of us can choose how we want to age. That means replacing old models that don't work with new ones that do and updating those that do work so they continue to work in the future. That's what disrupting aging is all about.

Aging's Four Freedoms

On January 6, 1941, the eve of the United States' entry into World War II, President Franklin Delano Roosevelt stood before a joint session of Congress to deliver his annual State of the Union address. In that speech Roosevelt argued for an end to the isolationist policies that grew out of World War I and offered a new ideology based on four freedoms: freedom of speech, freedom of worship, freedom from want, and freedom from fear. Roosevelt's four freedoms became a rallying cry to garner public support for America's involvement in World War II. They resonated with the American people as a statement of the country's underlying values, and to this day Roosevelt's four freedoms still ring true as the basic values that define American life and examples of American exceptionalism.

In much the same way that Roosevelt's four freedoms inspired America to wake up and realize what was happening in the world and to act, I have identified Four Freedoms of Aging that will define a new vision for living and aging in America and inspire us to disrupt aging, thus making that vision a reality.

1. *Freedom to Choose* how and where you want to live as you age. When it comes to aging, there is no one-size-fits-all solution. If you want to follow a traditional path to retirement, you should be able to do that. If you want an active, engaged life, you should have options to pursue that as well.

Whether you want to continue living in your own home as you get older, move to a retirement community, or live in an institutional setting, those options should all be available to you. It's all about having options available that allow you to choose how you live and age.

2. *Freedom to Earn.* A key part of the retirement model that most of us have grown up with is freedom from work. Today a key part of extended middle age is the freedom *to* work. Many of us want or need to continue earning a living and are searching for ways to make a difference in society through the work we do. This requires re-imagining work and breaking down both social and institutional barriers that stand in the way.

3. *Freedom to Learn.* Our world is changing so quickly. New technologies, new ways of communicating with each other, new ways of receiving and processing information—it's hard to keep up. If we want to stay engaged, involved, and productive during our extended middle age and beyond, we need to keep learning. If we want to continue working, we need to keep learning in order to keep our job skills up to date. We need to keep learning to avoid isolation. We need to keep learning for our own personal fulfillment and simply to enjoy life. But let's face it: the opportunities for us to keep learning diminish as we get older. In many cases they're just not there. As we disrupt aging, we will break down the barriers and create new opportunities to learn as we get older.

4. *Freedom to Pursue Happiness* by discovering and fulfilling our purpose. This is what it's really all about. Our longer lives give us an extraordinary opportunity to become the

people we have always wanted to be. No longer burdened by many of the day-to-day stresses that consumed our lives as we were advancing our careers and raising our kids, many of us are using our extended middle age to turn inward and focus on finding and fulfilling our purpose in life. We have the power to re-imagine our lives, to change its course and discover new ways to find fulfillment.

Civil rights leader A. Philip Randolph keenly observed, "Freedom is never given; it is won." So if we're going to win at attaining Aging's Four Freedoms, we have to work together to create a society where we have access to the care, information, and services we need to lead healthier lives with independence and dignity, where we have the financial resources and opportunities to match our longer life spans, and where we are seen as an integral and inspirational asset to society.

Winning these freedoms begins with each of us. We can't afford to sit on the sidelines and wait for someone else to win these freedoms for us; we have to do it for ourselves. It's time to tell our stories—what we believe and what we can do. So in conversations with your family and friends, what beliefs will you challenge? We need to change both the culture and the infrastructure of aging—the systems, programs, products, and services that we encounter every day. In your life and in your work, what solutions will you spark? In everything that you do, think about what new possibilities you can create for yourself and others.

What will you do to disrupt aging?

Disrupt Aging is our rallying cry to create a new vision of living and aging in the twenty-first century. Our new vision

is of a world in which aging is not about decline; it's about growth. It doesn't present only challenges; it creates new opportunities. And older people are not burdens; they are contributors.

I truly believe that age and experience can expand life's possibilities for every member of our society. When we disrupt aging and embrace it as something to look forward to instead of something to fear, we can begin to discover our real possibilities for becoming the person we always wanted to be and to build a society where all people are valued for who they are, not judged by how old they are.

JOIN THE CONVERSATION

I wrote this book to jumpstart a national movement to change the conversation in this country around what it means to grow older. I invite you to join the conversation on Facebook and on Twitter at #DisruptAging. Tell us what you are doing to disrupt aging and what aspects of society you think need to be disrupted.

I also encourage you to visit www.aarp.org/disruptaging to learn how other people are disrupting aging, to share your story, to get tips and ideas on how to disrupt aging, and to connect with other disruptors of all ages.

TAKE ACTION

CHAPTER TWO

Own Your Age

The experiences that have gotten you to this moment in life make you who you are. Own them.

Take Stock

Reflect on the ideas you have about your age—both positive and negative.

- ✔ What words come to mind about your current age?

- ✔ Jot them down. Are there more positive or negative words?

- ✔ In what situations do you feel comfortable sharing your age? Why?

- ✔ Have you ever lied about your age? Why?

- ✔ Are you letting age-related concerns limit you in any parts of your life?

- ✔ Think of a time when you've owned your age. How does this make you feel?

Take Action

Don't let yourself be limited by expectations of what you should or should not be or do at a certain age.

- ✓ Be on the lookout for accidental ageist language around you.

- ✓ If you hear someone say, "I'm too old/young for that," get curious. Ask them why they feel that way.

- ✓ Identify someone—a friend, family member, someone in your community or even a celebrity— whose approach to owning their age you admire. What can you take from their experience and apply to your own life?

CHAPTER THREE
Design Your Life

What if we stopped asking, *"What* do I want to be?" and started asking, *"Who* do I want to be?" It's never too early (or too late) to ask these questions and design a life that fits who we are becoming.

Look Back

Take a look at where you have been and what you have learned along the way.

- ✔ What advice would you give to your younger self?

- ✔ When have you felt most at home? Where were you? Who were you with?

- ✔ What are you most proud of?

- ✔ What's the biggest risk you have taken? What did you learn about yourself from that?

Look Forward

Imagine yourself 5 years from now. What's next for you?

- ↗ Imagine your future life. What do you see for yourself?

- ↗ Take a walk in your future neighborhood. What's around you?

- ↗ It's 3 P.M. on a weekday. What are you doing?

- ↗ Set your future dinner table. Who is joining you for dinner?

- ↗ How is your future life different from what it is today? How is it the same?

CHAPTER 4

Take Control of Your Health

What Matters Most to Your Health?

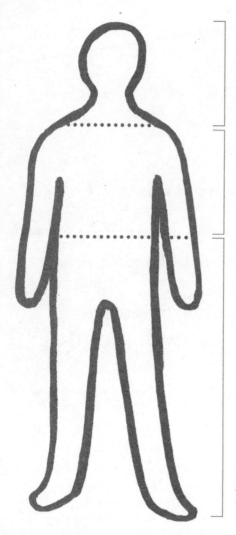

20% Genes

20% Health Care

60% Everyday Choices

The Boston Foundation and the
New England Healthcare Institute.
*Healthy People in a Healthy Economy:
A Blueprint for Action in Massachu-
setts.* Cambridge, MA: New England
Healthcare Institute, 2009.

Genes

Do you know what health risks and strengths run in your family? In this case, knowledge really is power.

- ✔ What genetic health gifts have been passed down to you?

- ✔ What conditions run in your family that worry you? How has your family handled these?

- ✔ Do you see any of these conditions showing up in your own health? Given that, what could you do to take control of your care?

- ✔ Do your doctors know your full genetic picture? What else do they need to know when considering preventive care and treatment options?

- ✔ Have you shared your family's health history with your children? What do they need to know to make strong decisions for themselves?

Health Care

Are you getting the health care you deserve? Bringing a consumer mindset to care decisions can make a big difference to your wallet and your wellness.

- ✔ Do you have the right care providers for your needs today, or have you outgrown them?

- ✔ Are you prepared for your doctor visits? Do you have a system for keeping track of your personal health history and questions you want to ask?

- ✔ Do you feel comfortable talking to your doctor? Do you feel rushed through visits? Or really listened to?

- ✔ What if you put the same energy into selecting a doctor as buying a car? What might you do differently?

Everyday Choices

Our daily choices shape our health more than any other factor. How can you make small changes that add up to big improvements?

- ✔ Reflect on what healthy living means to you—your own definition that fits your life today.

- ✔ What's one everyday choice or health habit that you are proud of? How did you build this into your routine?

- ✔ What's one small thing you'd like to change about your everyday health? What's the very next step you can take toward that goal?

- ✔ Don't go it alone! Who can you lean on to help you stay on track and meet your health goals?

CHAPTER 5

Choose Where You Live

Your zip code shapes your destiny.

From who your friends are, to your daily routines, to where you go for everything from the hair salon to the hospital. Asking these questions now will help you make the most out of where you live—today and tomorrow.

- ✔ How well does where you live suit you today?

- ✔ Is it where you want to be as you get older?

- ✔ Are there things to do now that will make your home more age-friendly?

- ✔ Or is there a move in your future?

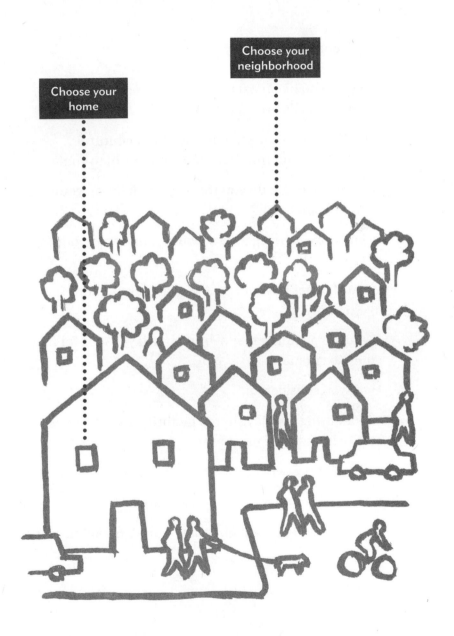

Choose Your Home

- What do you like most about your home today? What do you like the least?

- Will these factors matter as much in the future? What new things might become important to you?

- How much longer do you think you will live in your current home?

- If you broke your leg today, would your home work for you?

- What changes in your home would make it more age-friendly?

- If you are planning to move, what will you look for in your next home?

- Have you considered:

  - Cohousing to enjoy shared facilities and activities with friends and neighbors?

  - Connecting with others through virtual villages?

  - Sharing your house with roommates?

  - Renting rooms through online rental marketplaces?

Choose Your Neighborhood

🗸 Do you feel welcome in your neighborhood? Happy?

🗸 What kind of relationship do you have with your neighbors? Do you have friends nearby?

🗸 Are there opportunities to get involved in your neighborhood? To help out and be helped?

🗸 Do you see people of different ages out and about in your neighborhood? Do you interact with them?

🗸 Are the services you need easily accessible to you?

🗸 How would you handle a change in mobility? How would you get around?

🗸 Can you afford to keep living in your neighborhood? Can you afford to move?

🗸 If you were to move, what would you look for in your next neighborhood? Cost of living? Proximity to family and friends? Access to shops and services? Public transit? Climate?

CHAPTER 6

Finance Your Future

Our relationship to money, savings, and planning needs to catch up to the realities of aging—we are living longer, and with very different financial supports than our parents' generation. The old retirement model is out of date. It's time to create a new one that enables us to live the lives we choose for ourselves.

The Old Way: Planning for Retirement

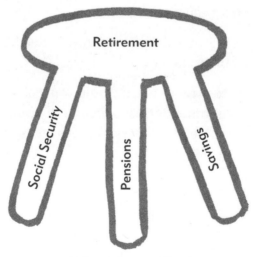

A Three-Legged Stool

The New Way: Achieving Financial Resilience

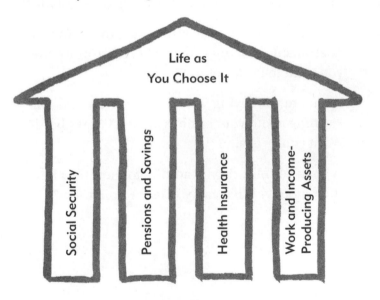

A Four-Pillar House

Your Mindset

Let's look at your relationship to money, savings, and planning. Think about the emotions financial planning triggers for you.

- How does planning for your financial future make you feel? Excited? Afraid? Stressed?

- What was the "story" of money in your family growing up? What did money mean to your family?

- Do you see any of these attitudes show up in your relationship to money today? Are there any patterns you want to leave behind?

- What are you saving for right now? What are you learning about your savings habits? What's hard? What comes easily?

- Who in your life do you admire for how they handle their money? What can you learn from them?

Your Plan

Think about what your life will look like ten years from today and whether you have a vision for your future activities, habits, interests, and relationships.

- Have you thought about how to pay for this future? Are you relying on Social Security? On savings? On generating ongoing income?

- Have you thought about how you will handle big ticket expenses—from getting sick to supporting family members?

- Will you be working in twenty years? Will you be in the same career? What can you be doing now to create more choices in the future?

- Where will you turn in an emergency?

- Do you have assets (e.g., house, car, etc.) that can produce additional income? How will you put them to use?

CHAPTER 7
Put Your Experience to Work

What will "work" look like for you ten years from now? What will be most important to you? To get clear on what this could look like, here are some questions to help get you going.

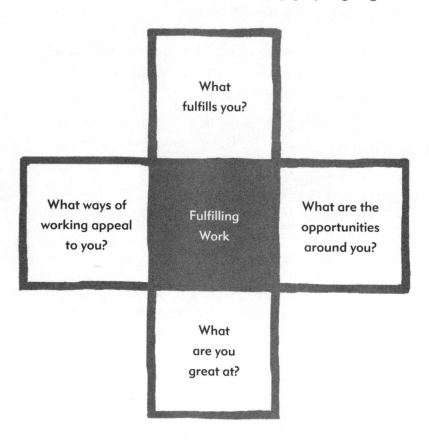

What fulfills you?
What fuels you—both personally and professionally? Where do you get joy? What activities give you energy (e.g., problem solving, facilitating groups, being there when people need you)?

What are you great at?
What are your skills? What are you known for excelling at? Think about talents that show up at home (e.g., cooking, storytelling, organization) and at work (e.g., teaching, plumbing, customer service).

What ways of working appeal to you?
Full time? Part time? Seasonal? Consultant? Volunteer? Mentor?

What are the opportunities around you?
How does your picture of what you want overlap with the opportunities around you? What kind of work is in demand? What's needed most? Who is doing work that calls to you?

LEARN MORE

RESOURCES

Chapter 1

Carstensen, Laura L., Ph.D. *A Long Bright Future: Happiness, Health, and Financial Security in an Age of Increased Longevity.* New York: Public Affairs, 2011.

Dychtwald, Ken, and Daniel J. Kadlec. *The Power Years: A User's Guide to the Rest of Your Life.* John Wiley & Sons, Inc., 2005.

Freedman, Marc. *The Big Shift: Navigating the New Stage Beyond Midlife.* New York: Public Affairs, 2011.

Irving, Paul H. *The Upside of Aging: How Long Life Is Changing the World of Health, Work, Innovation, Policy and Purpose.* Hoboken, NJ: John Wiley & Sons, Inc., 2014.

Lawrence-Lightfoot, Sara. *The Third Chapter: Passion, Risk, and Adventure in the 25 Years after 50.* New York: Sarah Crichton Books, 2009.

Chapter 2

Langer, Ellen J., Ph.D. *Counter Clockwise: Mindful Health and the Power of Possibility.* New York: Ballantine Books, 2009.

Thomas, Bill, M.D. *Second Wind: Navigating the Passage to a Slower, Deeper, and More Connected Life.* New York: Simon & Schuster, March 2015.

Chapter 3

Astor, Bart. *Roadmap for the Rest of Your Life: Smart Choices about Money, Health, Work, Lifestyle . . . and Pursuing Your Dreams.* Hoboken, NJ: John Wiley & Sons, Inc./AARP, 2013.

Cohen, Gene D., M.D., Ph.D. *The Creative Age: Awakening Human Potential in the Second Half of Life.* New York: Avon Books, 2000.

Huffington, Arianna. *Thrive: The Third Metric to Redefining Success and Creating a Life of Well-Being, Wisdom and Wonder.* New York: Harmony Books, 2014.

Leider, Richard J. and Alan M. Webber. *Life Reimagined: Discovering Your New Life Possibilities.* San Francisco: Berrett-Koehler Publishers, Inc./AARP, 2013.

Lucy, Robb. *Legacies Aren't Just for Dead People: Discover Happiness and a Meaningful Life by Creating and Enjoying Your Legacies Now!* Engage Communications, Inc., 2015.

Chapter 4

Barry, Patricia. *Medicare for Dummies.* Hoboken, NJ: John Wiley & Sons, Inc./AARP, 2014.

Langer, Ellen J., Ph.D. *Mindfulness: 25th Anniversary Edition.* Philadelphia: Da Capo Press, 2014.

Yagoda, Lisa, and Nicole Duritz (with Joan Friedman). *Affordable Care Act for Dummies.* Hoboken, NJ: John Wiley & Sons, Inc./AARP, 2014.

Chapter 5

Buettner, Dan. *The Blue Zones: Lessons for Living Longer from the People Who've Lived the Longest.* Washington, DC: The National Geographic Society, 2008.

In April 2015 the AARP Public Policy Institute launched the AARP Livability Index to help people determine how well their communities are meeting their current and future needs. Go to www.aarp.org/livabilityindex and type in your zip code to see how your community compares with others in terms of the livability factors that are important to you.

Chapter 6

Peterson, Jonathan. *Social Security for Dummies.* Hoboken, NJ: John Wiley & Sons, Inc./AARP, 2014.

Schwab-Pomerantz, Carrie. *The Charles Schwab Guide to Finances after 50: Answers to Your Most Important Money Questions.* New York: Crown Business, 2014.

Chapter 7

Cappelli, Peter, and Bill Novelli. *Managing the Older Worker: How to Prepare for the New Organizational Order.* Boston, MA: Harvard Business Review Press, 2010.

Leider, Richard, and David A. Shapiro. *Work Reimagined: Uncover Your Calling.* San Francisco: Berrett-Koehler Publishers, Inc./ AARP, 2015.

ONLINE RESOURCES

Disruptaging.aarp
AARP.org
ChangingAging.org
Agelab.mit.edu
huffingtonpost.com/50/
aging2.com
bigthink.com
LifeReimagined.org

ACKNOWLEDGMENTS

Just as it takes more than one person to disrupt aging in America, it has taken more than one person to make this book possible. I am grateful to the many people who contributed their talent, expertise, experience, and wisdom to bring this book to life. Although I can't mention them all, I would like to recognize a few.

After I took over as CEO of AARP in September 2014, I sat down with my speechwriter, Boe Workman, and our then chief communications officer, Kevin Donnellan (now AARP chief of staff), to discuss my first big speech at our National Event and Expo. Our discussion turned to what I wanted to accomplish as CEO. I said that if I could achieve only one thing as CEO of AARP, it would be to change the conversation in this country about what it means to grow older. The response to that speech, which we titled "Disrupt Aging," was so overwhelming that we decided to do this book. Boe and Kevin have been instrumental in this project from the beginning. I am deeply indebted to them for their hard work, support, and unwavering belief in *Disrupt Aging*. As my collaborator and writing partner, Boe did much of the hard work on this project. He and Kevin helped to frame the ideas and persisted in making sure we talked about these extremely complicated social issues in a very personal way.

I am also indebted to Colleen Lawrie, my editor at Public-Affairs. She is not only a skilled editor who knows how to make a book better, but her enthusiasm for the project and growing interest in the subject matter also inspired us to keep pushing forward to discover new insights. My thanks also go to PublicAffairs publisher Clive Priddle, who really wanted to do this project and whose wholehearted support kept us on track and on schedule. I am also grateful to his team at PublicAffairs: associate publisher Jaime Leifer, production manager Melissa Raymond, and all those involved in this project.

This book could not have been done without the help and support of my many talented and dedicated colleagues at AARP. Victoria Sackett provided valuable research assistance and read and commented on drafts, as did David Albee, Debra Whitman, and Leslie Nettleford. My thanks also go to Terri Greene and Monica Widoff, my valuable assistants who helped manage the demands of my schedule to keep me on track; to Myrna Blyth and Jodi Lipson in AARP Publications; to my colleagues on the executive team and the AARP board of directors for their support and encouragement; and to all the members of our Disrupt Aging team at AARP, led by Barbara Shipley, who are working every day to discover new ways to disrupt aging so more people can choose how they want to live and age.

I would also like to thank my trusted advisers at SYPartners —Keith Yamashita, Jessica Orkin, and Nicolas Maitret—for their counsel and advice. And I thank Belinda Lanks, Andrew Hearst, and Tony Vuong for the support they provided to the project.

I have also been encouraged by the support of those in the aging community. These leaders in the fight to help us all age better and to realize the societal impact of an aging America have accepted the idea of *Disrupt Aging* with open arms.

I could not have written this book without the support and encouragement of my family. To my husband, Frank, and my children, Christian and Nicole, I am forever thankful.

Finally, I am grateful to all of those people who are out there disrupting aging every day, especially those whose stories are included in this book. You are the true disruptors who are becoming the new role models for growing older. You are the people who make *Disrupt Aging* come to life, each in your own way. Without you, *Disrupt Aging* would be just another slogan. But with you, *Disrupt Aging* is a rallying cry for all of us to challenge outdated beliefs and stereotypes and spark new solutions so more people can choose how we want to live and age.

NOTES

Introduction: Why Disrupt Aging?

7   *the public largely holds an aspirational model of aging.* E. Lindland, M. Fond, A. Haydon, and N. Kendall-Taylor, *Gauging Aging: Mapping the Gaps Between Expert and Public Understandings of Aging in America* (Washington, DC: FrameWorks Institute, 2015). The other aging organizations included the American Society on Aging (ASA), the American Federation for Aging Research, the American Geriatrics Society, the Gerontological Society of America, the National Council on Aging, and the National Hispanic Council on Aging.

7   *". . . brings new opportunities and challenges for individuals and society."* Ibid., 6.

Chapter 1: The New Reality of Aging

13 *everyone who wants to be on the Internet is connected.* Jeffrey Cole, director of the Center for the Digital Future, Annenberg School for Communication and Journalism, University of Southern California, Los Angeles, CA, presentation at AARP's Ideas @ 50+ National Event & Expo, San Diego, CA, July 9, 2014.

13 *years to average life expectancy in the last century.* John W. Rowe and Robert L. Kahn, *Successful Aging* (New York: Pantheon Books, 1998).

13 *expect to live about nineteen more years.* National Center for Health Statistics, "NCHS Data Brief," no. 168 (October 2014), www .cdc.gov/nchs/data/databriefs/db168.pdf.

14 *heart disease, stroke, cancer, diabetes—became the major illnesses.* J. F. Fries, *Living Well* (Reading, MA: Perseus Books, 2004).

14 *would benefit both them and society.* J. F. Fries, "Aging, Natural Death, and the Compression of Morbidity," *New England Journal of Medicine* 303, no. 3 (July 17, 1980): 130–135.

16 *No group had been so ignored as older people were then.* Lewis Mumford, *The City in History: Its Origins, Its Transformations, and Its Prospects* (New York: Harcourt Brace Jovanovich, 1961).

17 *workforce was covered by a defined-benefit pension plan.* Employee Benefit Research Institute, "FAQs About Retirement Issues," www.ebri.org/publications/benfaq/index.cfm?fa=ret faq14.

22 *Black women, on average, do not live as long as white women.* National Center for Health Statistics, "NCHS Data Brief."

22 *and less in home equity than white non-Hispanics.* Centers for Disease Control and Prevention, "CDC Health Disparities and Inequalities Report—United States, 2013," www.cdc.gov/mmwr/pdf/other/su6203.

23 *life expectancy depending upon where one lives within the county.* Deb Whitman, "Not Everyone Is Living Longer," http://blog.aarp.org/2014/06/01/not-everyone-is-living-longer.

24 *will increasingly be a defining factor in the new reality of aging.* Guy Garcia, *The New Mainstream: How the Muilticultural Consumer Is Transforming American Business* (New York: Harper Business: 2005).

25 *larger than that of any country except the United States and China.* Oxford Economics, *The Longevity Economy: Generating Economic Growth and New Opportunities for Business* (Washington, DC: AARP, 2012).

25 *the fastest growing segment of Facebook users.* Cole, presentation at AARP's Ideas @ 50+ National Event & Expo.

31 *"the true wealth of nations."* Theodore Roszak, *America the Wise: Longevity, Revolution and the True Wealth of Nations* (New York: Houghton Mifflin, 1998).

Chapter 2: Own Your Age

34 *Satchel Paige was different, in more ways than one.* "Satchel

Paige Biography," Biography.com, www.biography.com/people/
satchel-paige-9431917.

39   *"I'm a hundred and four ... AND A HALF!"* Larry Miller, "Levels of
Aging," comedy routine. Reprinted with permission from Larry
Miller, November 11, 2015.

41   *living the life she wants to live as she gets older.* Rita Moreno, *Rita
Moreno: A Memoir* (New York: Penguin Group, Celebra, 2013).

41   *another perspective on this in her book,* Counterclockwise, Ellen
J. Langer, *Counterclockwise: Mindful Health and the Power of
Possibility* (New York: Ballantine Books, 2009).

43   *you could receive was a letter from Horace.* William Geist, *The Big
Five-Oh!: Facing, Fearing, and Fighting Fifty* (New York: Quill,
1998)

45   *"determined, dedicated and disciplined to be fit."* Alexandra Siffer-
lin. "Q&A: World's Oldest Performing Female Body Builder,"
Time, May 30, 2013, http://healthland.time.com/2013/05/30/qa
-worlds-oldest-performing-female-bodybuilder.

46   *"But I've learned a lot."* "99-Year-Old Agua Dulce Woman Graduates Friday from COC," SCVNews.com, June 3, 2015, http://scv
news.com/2015/06/03/99-year-old-agua-dulce-woman-gradu
ates-friday-from-coc.

46   *something she had to do for herself.* John Chadwick, "Grammy-
Winning Singer Returns to Rutgers for Degree," Rutgers Today,
April 16, 2015, http://news.rutgers.edu/feature/grammy-winning
-singer-returns-rutgers-degree/20150416#.VoCyrUorJkg.

48   *the average person doesn't become old until turning seventy-four.*
Pew Research Center. "Growing Old in America: Expectations
vs. Reality," www.newsocialtrends.org/2009/06/29/growing_old
_in_america_expectations_vs_reality.

Chapter 3: Design Your Life

54   *"the most powerful blog in the world."* "Arianna Huffington biography," Biography.com, www.biography.com/people/arianna
-huffington-21216537.

59   *opportunities for growth, development, and creativity.* Gene D.

Cohen, *The Creative Age: Awakening Human Potential in the Second Half of Life* (New York: Avon Books, 2000).

61 *"free to be and do whatever you want to."* Dorkys Ramos, "Oprah on Getting Older: 'The Absolute Best Part Is Being Able to Be Free," *Oprah Magazine,* May 2014, www.bet.com/news/lifestyle /2014/04/14/oprah-on-getting-older-the-absolute-best-part-is -being-able-to-be-free.html.

62 *creating and enjoying our legacies now.* Robb Lucy, *Legacies Aren't Just for Dead People: Discover Happiness and a Meaningful Life by Creating and Enjoying Your Legacies* (Vancouver, B.C.: Engage Communications, Inc., 2015), 17.

63 *"'Your problem is that you don't know healthy people.'"* This is from an internal AARP document generated from research into the AARP archives and the personal papers of Dr. Ethel Percy Andrus.

67 *"We can't allow these children to die like this."* Floyd Hammer and Kathy Hamilton, "The History of Outreach, Inc.," www.out reachprogram.org.

69 *"I just don't know what I want to do."* Scott Strain, phone interview with authors, October 29, 2015.

71 *a sense of purpose, and feeling like you belong.* Richard Leider, "Meaning Really Matters: The MetLife Study on How Purpose Is Recession Proof and Age-Proof," MetLife Mature Market Institute, July 2010.

Chapter 4: Take Control of Your Health

75 *20 percent is due to the medical care we receive.* The Boston Foundation and the New England Healthcare Institute, *Healthy People in a Healthy Economy: A Blueprint for Action in Massachusetts* (Cambridge, MA: New England Healthcare Institute, 2009), www .tbf.org/tbf/56/hphe/-/media/71D60849236E470D8FED6D67FE 9BEEDA.pdf.

75 *you won't see the effects until you get older.* Duane Alexander, L. Hightower, "Osteoporosis: Pediatric Disease with Geriatric Consequences," *Orthopedic Nursing* 19, no. 5 (September–October 2000): 59–62.

76   *higher than Norway, the next highest per capita spender.* Kaiser Family Foundation, "Peterson-Kaiser Health System Tracker," www.healthsystemtracker.org/chart-collection/how-does -health-spending-in-the-u-s-compare-to-other-countries.

77   *in terms of quality, access, and efficiency.* K. Davis, K. Stremlkis, D. Squires, and C. Schoen, *Mirror, Mirror on the Wall, 2014 Update: How the Performance of the U.S. Health Care System Compares Internationally* (The Commonwealth Fund, June 2014), www .commonwealthfund.org/publications/fund-reports/2014/jun/ mirror-mirror.

78   *"and that experiment is failing us."* Atul Gawande, *Being Mortal: Medicine and What Matters in the End* (New York: Metropolitan Books, Henry Holt and Company, 2014).

79   *defined in different ways by different entities.* R. Lavizzo-Mourey and A. Plough, *We're All in This Together: Improving America's Health by Taking Action and Measuring Programs* (Washington, DC: Robert Wood Johnson Foundation, 2015).

83   *preventive screenings, and nutrition assessments.* Bill Walsh, "America's Evolution Toward Wellness," *Generations: The Journal of the American Society on Aging* 39, no. 1 (Spring 2015): 23– 29, 24.

83   *most addressing fitness or chronic illness.* Ibid.

83   *more employees now have wellness programs.* Paul H. Keckley, and Sheryl Coughlin, *Breaking Constraints: Can Incentives Change Consumer Health Choices?* (San Francisco, CA: Deloitte University Press, 2013), http://dupress.com/articles/breaking -constraints.

84   *preventive service such as a mammogram, flu shot, or wellness visit.* Laura Skopec and Benjamin D. Sommers, "Affordable Care Act Extended Free Preventive Care to 71 Million Americans with Private Health Insurance," US Department of Health and Human Services, March 18, 2013, www.hhs.gov/news/press /2013pres/03/201303118a.html.

85   *"making these changes from fear of dying to the joy of living."* Dean Ornish, "It's Time to Embrace Lifestyle Medicine," *Time,* February–March 2015, 97.

88   *now have coverage under the ACA.* US Department of Health and Human Services, *Fact Sheet: The Affordable Care Act Is Working,* June 24, 2015, www.hhs.gov/healthcare/facts-and-features/fact -sheets/aca-is-working/index.html.

89   *save one hundred thousand lives each year.* Partnership for Prevention, "Preventive Care: A National Profile on Use, Disparities, and Health Benefits," Robert Wood Johnson Foundation, August 2007, www.rwjf.org/en/library/research/2007/08/ preventive-care-national-profile-on-use.html.

89   *in efforts to control costs, are cutting geriatrics programs.* The American Geriatrics Society, Data Center, www.americangeri atrics.org/advocacy_public_policy/gwps/gwps_data_center/ practice_of_geriatrics.

91   *"The future is here. It's just not evenly distributed yet,"* "Broadband Blues," *Economist,* June 21, 2001, www.economist.com/node /666610.

91   *plans to get into brain health in the future.* Walsh, "America's Evolution Toward Wellness."

91   *information technology, robotics, genetics, usership, and service enablers.* Joseph F. Coughlin, "Disruptive Demography: The New Business of Old Age," in *The Upside of Aging: How Long Life is Changing the World of Health, Work, Innovation, Policy and Purpose,* ed. Paul H. Irving, 51–62 (Hoboken, NJ: John Wiley & Sons, Inc., 2014)

92   *or heart rate monitoring while in your car.* Walsh, "America's Evolution Toward Wellness."

92   *timely alerts and immediate access to information.* AARP, Real Possibilities Project, "Building a Better Tracker: Older Consumers Weigh in on Activity and Sleep Monitoring Devices," July 14, 2015, www.aarp.org/content/dam/aarp/home-and-family/ personal-technology/2015-07/innovation-50-project-catalyst -tracker-study-AARP.pdf.

96   *"and those who will need caregivers."* Rosalynn Carter, "Remarks Accepting Honorary Chair of LAST ACTS," February 13, 1997, http://gos.sbc.edu/c/carter.html.

96   *long-term care lasting ninety days or longer.* Genworth, "Gen-

worth 2012 Cost of Care Survey," 2012, www.genworth.com/dam/Americas/US/PDFs/Consumer/corporate/coc_12.pdf.

96   *productivity to American businesses—mostly in lost time.* AARP and the National Alliance for Caregiving, "Caregiving in the U.S. 2015," June 2015, www.caregiving.org/wp-content/uploads/2015/05/2015_CaregivingintheUS_Executive-Summary-June-4_WEB.pdf.

97   *providing support for both their kids and their parents.* Ibid.

97   *a long-term-care system in drastic need of change.* US Census Bureau, "American Householders Are Getting Older," Census Bureau Reports, November 15, 2012, www.census.gov/newsroom/releases/archives/families_households/cb12-216.html.

98   *CareLinx, Inc., founded by Sherwin Sheik.* CareLinx, "About CareLinx," www.carelinx.com/about. Note: CareLinx was a winner of one of AARP's Live Pitch events mentioned earlier.

99   *responses for patients being discharged from the hospital and in other situations.* Miguel Helft, "How the Tech Elite Plans to Reinvent Senior Care," *Forbes*, April 2, 2015, www.forbes.com/sites/miguelhelft/2015/04/02/how-the-tech-elite-plans-to-reinvent-senior-care.

100   *unless we find new ways to control the disease.* Alzheimer's Association, "Changing the Trajectory of Alzheimer's Disease: How a Treatment by 2025 Saves Lives and Dollars," 2015, www.alz.org/trajectory.

100   *save more than $440 billion in caregiving costs.* Michael D. Hurd, Paco Martorell, Adeline Delavande, Kathleen J. Mullen, and Kenneth M. Langa, "Monetary Costs of Dementia in the United States," *New England Journal of Medicine* 368, no. 14 (April 4, 2013): 1326–1334.

101   *"I just kept getting older and couldn't help it."* Michel Allard, Victor Lebre, and Jean-Marie Robine, *Jeanne Calment: From Van Gogh's Time to Ours, 122 Extraordinary Years* (New York: W. H. Freeman and Company, 1994).

102   *exercise of mind and body, and engagement in life.* John W. Rowe and Robert L. Kahn, *Successful Aging* (New York: Pantheon Books, 1998).

Chapter 5: Choose Where You Live

104   *the long redevelopment project with Habitat.* Laura Ingles, "Extreme Makeover: Habitat for Humanity Turns Trailer Parks into Town Centers," August 7, 2012, http://www.c-ville.com.

105   *report on the Best Cities for Successful Aging.* Anusuya Chatterjee and Jacque King, *Best Cities for Successful Aging 2014* (Santa Monica, CA: Milken Institute, 2014), http://successfulaging.milkenin stitute.org/2014/best-cities-for-successful-aging-report-2014.pdf.

109   *clear sense of purpose; and develop strong social networks.* Dan Buettner, *The Blue Zones: Lessons for Living Longer from the People Who've Lived the Longest* (Washington, DC: The National Geographic Society, 2008).

110   *"the Vitality Project. It's made me feel better about Albert Lea and America."* Dan Buettner, "The Minnesota Miracle," *AARP: The Magazine,* January/February 2010, www.aarp.org/health/ longevity/info-01-2010/minnesota_miracle.html.

116   *no public transportation within a ten-minute walk from their home.* Linda Bailey, *Aging Americans: Stranded Without Options,* Surface Transportation Policy Project (AARP and American Public Transportation Association, April 2004).

118   *reduce injuries, deaths, and automobile crashes.* National Complete Streets Coalition, "Presentation: The Many Benefits of Complete Streets," March 2015, www.smartgrowthamerica.org/ complete-streets.

118   *getting from one curb to the other before the light changed was a challenge.* A. Barry Rand, "Making Safe Streets a Real Possibility," AARP Bulletin, April 2014.

118   *"upgraded crosswalks and shorter crossing distances for pedestrians."* Ibid.

120   *"just a lovely feeling, having them nearby."* Amy Crawford, "Why a Boston Suburb Combined Its High School and Senior Center," CityLab, October 12, 2015, www.citylab.com/work/2015/10/why -this-town-combined-its-high-school-and-senior-center/410149.

120   *a for-profit telemedicine support program, and it's become hugely successful.* Liza Kaufman Hogan, "3 Innovative Ways to

Age in Place," *Forbes*, June 12, 2014. www.forbes.com/sites/next avenue/2014/06/12/3-innovative-ways-to-age-in-place.

123   *and another 120 are on the drawing board.* Constance Gustkenov, "Retirees Turn to Virtual Villages for Mutual Support," *New York Times*, November 28, 2014, www.nytimes.com/2014/11/29/your -money/retirees-turn-to-virtual-villages-for-mutual-support .html.

124   *It was just what she was looking for.* Brenda Krause Eheart, interview with authors, September 19, 2015. She also received a 2009 AARP Inspire Award.

126   *felt like he had found the perfect fit.* Bill Thomas, interview with authors, June 12, 2015.

Chapter 6: Finance Your Future

132   *that amount would provide an income of only $405 a month.* US Government Accountability Office, "Retirement Security: Most Households Approaching Retirement Have Low Savings," Report to the Ranking Member, Subcommittee on Primary Health and Retirement Security, Committee on Health, Education, Labor, and Pensions, US Senate, Washington, DC, May 2015.

132   *accumulated savings and investments of $250,000 or more.* Ruth Helman, Craig Copeland, and Jack VanDerhei, "The 2015 Retirement Confidence Survey: Having a Retirement Savings Plan a Key Factor in Americans' Retirement Confidence," EBRI Issue Brief, no. 413 (Employee Benefit Research Institute, April 2015), available at www.ebri.org. Of workers twenty-five and over, 22 percent are very confident of having enough money; 36 percent are somewhat confident; and 25 percent are not at all confident. More than half of all respondents said they had less than $25,000, and 28 percent had less than $1,000.

132   *no idea how much they should be saving.* Ibid.

134   *Today 15 percent of Americans live in poverty—the highest level since 1993.* US Census Bureau, "Income, Poverty and Health Insurance Coverage in the United States: 2013," September 16, 2014,

Release Number: CB14-169, www.census.gov/newsroom/press -releases/2014/cb14-169.html.

134 *income gains that typical American families made over the last ten years.* David Auerbach, "Accelerating Health Care Costs Wiping Out Much of Americans' Income Gains," RAND Corporation, September 8, 2011, www.rand.org/news/press/2011/09/08.html.

134 *so much debt that they can't afford to retire.* E. S. Browning, "Debt Hobbles Older Americans," *Wall Street Journal,* September 7, 2011, www.wsj.com/articles/SB100014240531119042334045764600 20958393028.

135 *financing their so-called retirement years.* Investor Protection Institute, "The College Debt/Retirement Savings Bind," September 17, 2015, www.iinvest.org/wp-content/uploads/2015/03/IPI_ Millennial_Survey_Findings_09-17-15.pdf.

136 *more likely to be targets of scams and frauds.* AARP, "2013 Retirement Confidence Survey: A Secondary Analysis of the Findings from Respondents Age 50+," May 2013, www.aarp.org/content /dam/aarp/research/surveys_statistics/general/2013/2013 -Retirement-Confidence-Survey-A-Secondary-Analysis-of-the -Findings-from-Respondents-Age-50-Plus-AARP-rsa-gen.pdf.

139 *28 percent average increase in the amount set aside for retirement.* Ron Lieber, "A Nudge to Save a Bit More for Retirement, Online Tools Can Encourage Greater Saving," *New York Times,* June 27, 2014, /www.nytimes.com/2014/06/28/your-money/for -retirement-online-tools-can-encourage-greater-saving.html ?_r=0.

142 *the number is continuing to decline.* Employee Benefit Research Institute, "FAQs About Benefits—Retirement Issues: What Are the Trends in U.S. Retirement Plans?" www.ebri.org/publications /benfaq/index.cfm?fa=retfaq14.

143 *and provided benefits to about 59 million people in 2014.* Alison Shelton, *Social Security: Who's Counting on It?* (AARP Public Policy Institute, August 6, 2015), www.aarp.org/ppi/info-2015/ social-security-who-is-counting-on-it.html.

144 *before your full retirement age (as early as age sixty-two).* US Social

Security Administration, "Fact Sheet: 2015 Social Security Changes," www.ssa.gov/news/press/factsheets/colafacts2015 .html.

144   *disability protections are valued at $329,000.* Jonathan Peterson, *Social Security for Dummies* (Hoboken, NJ: John Wiley & Sons, 2012).

144   *portable, guaranteed, universal, and protected against inflation.* Ibid.

144   *pay 79 percent of benefits and 73 percent of benefits in 2089.* Board of Trustees, Federal Old-Age and Survivors Insurance and Federal Disability Insurance Trust Funds. *The 2015 Annual Report of the Board of Trustees of the Federal Old-Age and Survivors Insurance and Disability Insurance Trust Funds* (Washington, DC: Social Security Administration, July 22, 2015), http://ssa.gov/ OACT/TR/2015/tr2015.pdf.

145   *(increase from $500 to $800 billion over the next decade).* The Henry J. Kaiser Family Foundation, "The Facts on Medicare Spending and Financing," July 24, 2015, http://kff.org/medicare /fact-sheet/medicare-spending-and-financing-fact-sheet.

147   *easy to open your home to someone for a profit.* Janice Tharaldson, interview with authors, September 19, 2015.

148   *this also helps them to remain socially active.* Airbnb, "Celebrating Airbnb's 60+ Host Community," July 30, 2015, http://blog .airbnb.com/celebrating-airbnbs-60-host-community.

148   *that it will grow to $355 billion by 2025.* PricewaterhouseCoopers, "Employee Financial Wellness Survey 2014 Results," April 2014, www.pwc.com/us/en/private-company-services/publications /assets/pwc-employee-financial-wellness-survey-2014-results .pdf.

148   *and one in four are fifty or over.* Maryalene La Ponsie, "How Retirees Can Make Money in the Sharing Economy," *U.S. News and World Report,* August 20, 2015, http://money.usnews.com /money/retirement/articles/2015/08/20/how-retirees-can -make-money-in-the-sharing-economy.

149   *"probably retire sooner rather than later."* Jeff Bertolucci, "6 Easy

Ways Retirees Can Cash in on the Sharing Economy," *Kiplinger's Retirement Report,* February 2015, www.kiplinger.com /printstory.php?pid=13368.

149   *charges $49 an hour to assemble IKEA furniture.* Amy Zipken, "The Sharing Economy Attracts Older Adults," *New York Times,* September 25, 2015, www.nytimes.com/2015/09/26/your-money/the -sharing-economy-attracts-older-adults.html?_r=2.

149   *"enjoy luxuries while paying just a portion of the costs."* Joan Voight, "Sharing-for-Cash: A New Way to Finance Retirement," CNBC, May 1, 2012, www.cnbc.com/id/46854427.

149   *about one-third are over fifty.* Bertolucci, "6 Easy Ways Retirees Can Cash in on the Sharing Economy."

152   *fraud affects about 10 percent of people to varying degrees.* Kate Rogers, "Someone Became an Identity Theft Victim Every 2 Seconds Last Year," *Fox Business,* February 5, 2014, www.fox business.com/personal-finance/2014/02/05/someone-became -identity-theft-victim-every-2-seconds-last-year.

153   *"that was about how much she was living on entirely."* Kai Stinch-combe, phone interview with authors, September 19, 2015.

Chapter 7: Put Your Experience to Work

159   *considered traditional retirement age, either out of choice or necessity.* Aon Hewitt and AARP, *The Business Case for Workers Age 50+: A Look at the Value of Experience 2015* (Washington, DC: AARP, March 2015), http://states.aarp.org/wp-content/uploads /2015/08/A-Business-Case-for-Older-Workers-Age-50-A-Look-at -the-Value-of-Experience.pdf.

159   *US employers reported difficulty in filling jobs.* Manpower Group, "2014 Talent Shortage Survey," www.manpowergroup.us/cam paigns/talent-shortage-2014.

162   *no longer a significant factor in the costs of hiring and retaining workers.* Hewitt and AARP, *The Business Case for Workers Age 50+.*

162   *the overall workforce is more productive.* Yurly Gorodnichenko, John Laitner, Jae Song, and Dimitriy Stolyarov, *Technological*

Progress and the Earnings of Older Workers (University of Michigan Retirement Research Center, October 2013).

162 *training related to computers and information/communication technology.* Towers Perrin and AARP, *Investing in Training 50+ Workers: A Talent Management Strategy, 2008* (Washington, DC: AARP, 2008).

163 *"we need both old and young working together."* Vivek Wadhwa, "There's No Age Requirement for Innovation," The Accelerators, *Wall Street Journal*, October 28, 2013, http://blogs.wsj.com /accelerators/2013/10/28/vivek-wadhwa-theres-no-age-require ment-for-innovation.

163 *"we need to solve the big problems that the world faces."* Ibid.

164 *availability of Social Security benefits and other pension and insurance systems than displacement.* Howard N. Fullerton, "Labor Force Participation: 75 Years of Change, 1950–98 and 1998–2025," *Monthly Labor Review* (December 1999): 3–12, www.bls.gov/mlr /1999/12/art1full.pdf.

164 *thus the economy grows, creating more jobs.* Hewitt and AARP, *The Business Case for Workers Age 50+.*

164 *older persons will increase the unemployment of youth.* Jonathan Gruber and David A. Wise, eds. *Social Security Programs and Retirement Around the World: The Relationship to Youth Employment* (Chicago: University of Chicago Press, 2010).

164 *conflicts would arise when younger supervisors manage older 64workers.* Peter Cappelli and Bill Novelli, *Managing the Older Worker: How to Prepare for the New Organizational Order* (Boston: Harvard Business Review Press, 2010).

166 *leads to increased productivity and business outcomes.* Suzanne J. Peterson and Barry K. Spiker, "Establishing the Positive Contributory Value of Older Workers: A Positive Psychology Perspective," *Organizational Dynamics* 34, no. 2 (2005): 153–167.

166 *there is a lot they still plan to accomplish.* AARP and GfK Roper, *Staying Ahead of the Curve 2013: The AARP Work and Career Study* (AARP, January 2014), www.aarp.org/content/dam/aarp/ research/surveys_statistics/general/2014/Staying-Ahead-of-the -Curve-2013-The-Work-and-Career-Study-AARP-res-gen.pdf.

168   *integrate work and personal life; fair treatment; and competitive compensation.* Monique Valcour, "Hitting the Intergenerational Sweet Spot," *Harvard Business Review,* May 27, 2013, https://hbr.org/2013/05/hitting-the-intergenerational.

168   *motivation and commitment long before the invention of the smartphone.* Ibid.

169   *maintain or improve productivity.* Christopher H. Loch, Fabian J. Sting, Nikolaus Bauer, and Helmut Mauermann, "How BMW Is Defusing the Demographic Time Bomb," *Harvard Business Review* 88, no. 3 (March 2010): 99–102.

169   *saving the company training and recruitment costs.* D. Piktialis, "Adaptations to an Aging Workforce: Innovative Responses by the Corporate Sector," *Generations* 31, no. 1 (Spring 2007): 76–82.

169   *"associate coaches" to train and mentor younger workers.* Steven Greenhouse, "The Age Premium: Retaining Older Workers," *New York Times,* May 14, 2014, www.nytimes.com/2014/05/15/business/retirementspecial/the-age-premium-retaining-older-workers.html.

170   *"The older staff picked it up immediately."* Kerry Hannon, "As Workers Delay Retirement, Some Bosses Become More Flexible," *New York Times,* August 21, 2015, www.nytimes.com/2015/08/22/your-money/delay-retirement-flexible-work-schedules.html.

171   *a reduced schedule if they want to continue working.* Hewitt and AARP, *The Business Case for Workers Age 50+.*

172   *an invaluable asset for quality of care and informal mentoring.* Ibid.

173   *benefit from the older workers' knowledge and experience.* Ibid.

173   *sessions for employees who are caregivers.* Ibid.

176   *reverse mentoring as a way to stay current.* Leslie Kwoh, "Reverse Mentoring Cracks Workplace: Top Managers Get Advice on Social Media, Workplace Issues from Young Workers," *Wall Street Journal,* November 28, 2011, www.wsj.com/articles/SB10001424052970203764804577060051461094004.

176   *"the keys to trends and information I wasn't being exposed to."* Stephanie Vozza, "Why a PayPal Executive Is Being Mentored by His Millennial Employees," *Fast Company,* September 23, 2015,

www.fastcompany.com/3051164/lessons-learned/why-a-paypal
-executive-is-being-mentored-by-his-millennial-employees.

177   *then went on to Columbia Business School.* Lester Strong, interview with authors, November 30, 2015.

178   *children in kindergarten through third grade in 211 schools across the country.* AARP Experience Corps, "Frequently Asked Questions," www.aarp.org/experience-corps/about-us/experience -corps-frequently-asked-questions.

178   *another 31 million are interested in doing so.* Civic Ventures. *Encore Career Choices: Purpose, Passion and a Paycheck in a Tough Economy.* A MetLife Foundation/Civic Ventures Report Based on Research by Penn Schoen Berland. 2011. http://www.encore.org/ files/EncoreCareerChoices.pdf.

178   *freedom to work, that is more indicative of the way we are aging today.* Marc Freedman. *Encore: Finding Work that Matters in the Second Half of Life* (New York: Public Affairs, August 2008).

179   *leading them to contemplate changes they had never considered before.* Anne Tergesen, "The Case for a Midlife 'Gap' Year," *Wall Street Journal,* December 8, 2013, www.wsj.com/articles/SB10001 42405270230464410457919193404594991.

179   *unretire a year or two later and return to work.* Nicole Maestas, "Back to Work: Expectations and Realizations of Work After Retirement," Rand Corporation working paper, April 2007, http:// www.rand.org/content/dam/rand/pubs/working_papers/2007/ RAND_WR196-2.pdf.

Chapter 8: Let's Change the Rules

185   *a potential 17 percent cost savings for Medicare among the oldest of the population.* Medstar Washington Hospital Center, "New Data Shows Home-Based Primary Care Lowers Medicare Costs for High-Risk Elders," August 4, 2014, www.medstarwashington .org/2014/08/04/new-data-shows-home-based-primary-care -lowers-medicare-costs-for-high-risk-elders/#q={}.

185   *The average Medicare benefit per enrollee was $12,179.* The Boards of Trustees, Federal Hospital Insurance and Federal

Supplementary Medical Insurance Trust Funds, "2015 Annual Report of the Boards of Trustees of the Federal Hospital Insurance and Federal Medical Insurance Trust Funds," Centers for Medicare and Medicaid Services, www.cms.gov/research -statistics-data-and-systems/statistics-trends-and-reports/ reportstrustfunds/downloads/tr2015.pdf.

187 *the economic value of their unpaid contributions at roughly $470 billion a year.* AARP and National Alliance for Caregiving, *Caregiving in the U.S.: 2015 Report* (Washington, DC: AARP Public Policy Institute, June 2014), www.aarp.org/content/dam/aarp/ ppi/2015/caregiving-in-the-united-states-2015-report-revised .pdf.

190 *Social Security kept over 22 million Americans of all ages out of poverty.* Mikki Waid, "Social Security Keeps Americans of All Ages Out of Poverty: State-Level Estimates, 2011–2103," AARP, July 20, 2015, www.aarp.org/ppi/info-2015/social-security-keeps -americans-of-all-ages-out-of-poverty.html.

190 *adults under thirty want to know it will be there when they retire.* Alicia Williams, "Social Security 80th Anniversary Survey Report," AARP, August 2015, www.aarp.org/SeguroSocial80.

191 *benefits will be cut by more than 20 percent in 2034.* Social Security Administration, *The 2015 Annual Report of the Board of Trustees of the Federal Old-Age and Survivors Insurance and Federal Disability Insurance Trust Funds* (Washington, DC: U.S. Government Publishing Office, 2015), www.ssa.gov/oact/TR/2015/ tr2015.pdf.

194 *so many people worry that they will outlive their money.* Employee Benefits Research Institute, "2014 RCS Fact Sheet #6," EBRI, http://ebri.org/pdf/surveys/rcs/2014/RCS14.FS-6.Prep-Ret .Final.pdf.

194 *of those who do, too many don't participate.* David John and Gary Koenig, *Workplace Retirement Plans Will Help Workers Build Economic Security* (AARP Public Policy Institute, October 2014), www.aarp.org/content/dam/aarp/ppi/2014-10/aarp-workplace -retirement-plans-build-economic-security.pdf.

195   *deduction for retirement savings, their participation rate is a whopping success.* Brigitte C. Madrian, *Retirement Saving Policy That Was Easy: The Importance of Auto Features in Promoting Retirement Savings* (AARP Public Policy Institute, October 2014), www.aarp.org/content/dam/aarp/ppi/2014-10/spotlight12 -importance-auto-features-promoting-retirement-savings -AARP-ppi-econ-sec.pdf.

195   *help people save more over time.* Ibid.

197   *having insufficient savings for their retirement years.* Alicia H. Munnell, Anthony Webb, and Wenliang Hou, *How Much Should People Save?* (Center for Retirement Research at Boston College, July 2014), http://crr.bc.edu/wp-content/uploads/2014/07/IB_14 -111.pdf.

199   *(only about 6 percent of households) have income from private annuities.* Richard W. Johnson, Leonard E. Burman, and Deborah I. Kobes, *Annuitized Wealth at Older Ages: Evidence from the Health and Retirement Study* (Washington, DC: The Urban Institute, 2004), www.urban.org/sites/default/files/alfresco/publica tion-pdfs/411000-Annuitized-Wealth-at-Older-Ages.PDF.

200   *financial exploitation is the fastest-growing form of elder abuse.* Wendy Fox-Grage, "Financial Abuse of Older Adults: AARP and American Bankers Association Foundation Partner to Tackle Growing Problem," AARP, August 27, 2015, http://blog .aarp.org/2015/08/27/financial-abuse-of-older-adults-aarp-and -american-bankers-association-foundation-partner-to-tackle -growing-problem.

201   *rely on services like payday lending rather than routine banking.* Federal Deposit Insurance Corporation, "2011 FDIC National Survey of Unbanked and Underbanked Households," September 2012, www.fdic.gov/householdsurvey/2012_unbankedreport.pdf.

202   *is now testing how to provide education to protect those customers.* Jilenne Gunther and Robert Neill, *Inspiring Case Examples: Age-Friendly Banking* (AARP, June 2014).

202   *does not provide access to funds or the ability to make transactions.* Ibid.

202   *banks in Oregon are now the second-largest reporter of elder abuse in the state.* Ibid.

205   *signaled on their LinkedIn profiles that they are interested in volunteering.* Omar Garriott, "Millions of LinkedIn Members Want to Volunteer Their Skills for Good" (infographic), LinkedIn, January 30, 2015, http://blog.linkedin.com/2015/01/30/millions-of-linkedin-members-want-to-volunteer-their-skills-for-good-infographic.

207   *a pedestrian is killed because of unsafe streets or crosswalks.* US Department of Transportation, National Highway Traffic Safety Administration (NHTSA), *Traffic Safety Facts 2012: Pedestrians* (Washington, DC: NHTSA; 2014), www-nrd.nhtsa.dot.gov/Pubs /811888.pdf/.

ABOUT THE AUTHOR

Jo Ann Jenkins is CEO of AARP, the world's largest nonprofit, nonpartisan membership organization dedicated to social change and helping people fifty and over to improve the quality of their lives. Jenkins was formerly the COO of the Library of Congress, where she received the 11th Annual Women in Technology Leadership Award and was a recipient of the Library of Congress Distinguished Service Award. She is a Malcolm Baldrige fellow, recipient of the 2013 Black Women's Agenda Economic Development Award, one of the *NonProfit Times*'s Power and Influence Top 50 for 2013 and 2014, and, in 2015, was named Non-Profit Influencer of the Year. Jenkins lives in northern Virginia.

PublicAffairs is a publishing house founded in 1997. It is a tribute to the standards, values, and flair of three persons who have served as mentors to countless reporters, writers, editors, and book people of all kinds, including me.

I. F. STONE, proprietor of *I. F. Stone's Weekly*, combined a commitment to the First Amendment with entrepreneurial zeal and reporting skill and became one of the great independent journalists in American history. At the age of eighty, Izzy published *The Trial of Socrates*, which was a national bestseller. He wrote the book after he taught himself ancient Greek.

BENJAMIN C. BRADLEE was for nearly thirty years the charismatic editorial leader of *The Washington Post*. It was Ben who gave the *Post* the range and courage to pursue such historic issues as Watergate. He supported his reporters with a tenacity that made them fearless and it is no accident that so many became authors of influential, best-selling books.

ROBERT L. BERNSTEIN, the chief executive of Random House for more than a quarter century, guided one of the nation's premier publishing houses. Bob was personally responsible for many books of political dissent and argument that challenged tyranny around the globe. He is also the founder and longtime chair of Human Rights Watch, one of the most respected human rights organizations in the world.

·   ·   ·

For fifty years, the banner of Public Affairs Press was carried by its owner Morris B. Schnapper, who published Gandhi, Nasser, Toynbee, Truman, and about 1,500 other authors. In 1983, Schnapper was described by *The Washington Post* as "a redoubtable gadfly." His legacy will endure in the books to come.

Peter Osnos, *Founder and Editor-at-Large*